"Scientific knowledge on the cosmic and on the biological evolution has become highly strengthened in recent decades. Evolutionary progress results from quite slow dynamic processes that reveal natural laws for permanent creation. Verschuuren's book can be expected to foster a harmonious integration of scientific facts together with religious beliefs into our orientational knowledge."

— Professor Werner Arber, Nobel Laureate in Medicine 1978, President of the Pontifical Academy of Sciences

"Gerard M. Verschuuren has done us all a favor by giving us a clear, faithful, and lucid survey of the Catholic position on evolution, avoiding all foolish extremes, and showing that real science and real Catholic faith not only have nothing to fear from each other, but are vital to illuminating one another."

— Mark P. Shea, apologetics speaker, senior content writer for www.catholicexchange.com, author of "Connecting the Dots" column in the *National Catholic Register*

"This is a well-written work that discusses the position of the Catholic Church with regard to the theory of evolution. The scientific explanations are exceptionally clear. Dr. Verschuuren makes fine use of modern sources and has produced a book that is to be praised and extensively read."

— The Most Rev. John B. McCormack, Bishop Emeritus, Diocese of Manchester, New Hampshire

"*God and Evolution* is a thoughtful, well-argued, and easy to read presentation of the conversation between science and faith. As Gerard Verschuuren argues, science and religion, or evolution and creation, are two windows that see the world from different perspectives which are not contradictory but complementary. Dr. Verschuuren documents the religious perspective with pertinent citations from Scripture, theologians, and philosophers. As an expert biologist, he convincingly makes the case for science."

— Francisco J. Ayala, Donald Bren Professor of Biological Sciences, University of California, Irvine, California; recipient of the 2010 Templeton Prize; Past President of the American Association for the Advancement of Science

# GOD *and*
# EVOLUTION?

# GOD *and* EVOLUTION?

## SCIENCE MEETS FAITH

Dr. Gerard M. Verschuuren

With a Foreword by Carlos A. Sevilla, SJ

*auline*
BOOKS & MEDIA
Boston

*Nihil Obstat:* Most Reverend John B. McCormack, Bishop Emeritus
Diocese of Manchester
April 11, 2012

Library of Congress Cataloging-in-Publication Data

Verschuuren, G. M. N. (Geert M. N.)
God and evolution? : science meets faith / Gerard M. Verschuuren ; with a foreword by Carlos A. Sevilla.
    p. cm.
Includes bibliographical references.
ISBN-13: 978-0-8198-3113-2
ISBN-10: 0-8198-3113-1
1. Evolution (Biology)--Religious aspects--Christianity. I. Title.
BX1795.E85V47 2012
                    231.7'652--dc23

Cover design by Rosana Usselmann

Cover photo: istockphoto.com / © Johan Swanepoel

Published by Pauline Books & Media, 50 Saint Pauls Avenue, Boston, MA 02130-3491

Printed in the U.S.A.

www.pauline.org

Pauline Books & Media is the publishing house of the Daughters of St. Paul, an international congregation of women religious serving the Church with the communications media.

1 2 3 4 5 6 7 8 9                                        16 15 14 13 12

*Dedicated to*
*Pope Benedict XVI,*
*the tireless defender of faith and reason,*
*and to all Catholics in search of the truth*

# Contents

# Acknowledgments

I wish to express special gratitude to the Most Rev. Carlos Sevilla, SJ, of the Diocese of Yakima; Francisco J. Ayala of the University of California at Irvine; Rev. Marcel Chappin of the Pontifical Gregorian University in Rome; John Jones of The Crossroad Publishing Company; Kenneth W. Kemp of the University of Saint Thomas; Peter Kreeft of Boston College; James McGhee of Saint Anselm's College; and Kenneth R. Miller of Brown University for helping me to improve the text of this book by their input, comments, and suggestions. They and many others make me realize that originality only consists in the capacity of forgetting about your sources.

# Foreword

Saint Paul was right on target in saying, "When I was a child, I spoke like a child, I thought like a child, I reasoned like a child; when I became an adult, I put an end to childish ways" (1 Cor 13:11). It's obvious that the challenges that led Saint Paul to make his statement were very different from those we as Catholics encounter today. Nonetheless, it remains true that our life of faith needs to be deepened and nourished as we grow older and mature.

For example, one of the more important challenges faced by many Catholic believers today is the seemingly opposite, if not apparently contradictory, approaches taken to evolution by our modern science-driven world and to what can be authentically and correctly presented to us as Catholic teaching about evolution.

This book by Dr. Verschuuren, an old friend of mine, will be a great resource and, I believe, a positive help to integrate a solid, scientific understanding of evolution with the most current teaching about evolution from the faith perspectives of our popes, especially John Paul II and Benedict XVI.

Dr. Verschuuren, an accomplished and respected scientist with expertise in many areas, is dedicated to the Church, its traditions, and its teachings. Although I cannot evaluate the full extent of the scientific data in Dr. Verschuuren's book—scientists have done that—I can assure its readers that the author has a very sound Catholic approach to God, creation, and evolution. The many well-chosen citations from Pope John Paul II and Pope Benedict XVI are, it seems to me, all the proof a reader should need of that fact.

This remarkable book brings together two powerful realities: the power of God and the power of science, without falling into the traps of creationism or evolutionism. As the book's arguments advance and the evidence mounts, the reader will gain a stronger and stronger sense of God's presence in this world. Step by step, we are brought forward into the awesome relationship between religion and science.

Although the book discusses complex scientific issues, the reader will comprehend them with relative ease because Dr. Verschuuren has the gift of explaining things clearly and compellingly. I am grateful to him for finding and bringing to life the right balance between religion and science. I can promise you this book is going to enrich your mind and deepen your faith. It is a must read, clear and concise, filled with biblical and scientific truths. I enjoyed the book enormously.

THE MOST REVEREND CARLOS A. SEVILLA, SJ
Bishop Emeritus of the Diocese of Yakima, WA

# Introduction

The question "Where do we come from?" is an issue of life or death. If evolution has the last word, then death is ultimately the end of the story. But if there is creation, then eternal life is the light at the end of the tunnel. No wonder the discussion keeps stirring our minds: Where do we come from? Are our roots in the animal world, or are we rooted in God? Or are both perhaps true? What should we teach at our schools? What should we preach in our churches? What should we believe as Catholics living in the twenty-first century? Should it be both evolution and creation, or just one of them? And as Catholic parents, what do we say to our children when they come home from school with stories about evolution?

Not long ago, many Catholics in the pews understood that evolution was somehow consistent with Church teaching. What has changed is not Church teaching, or evolutionary theory, but the fact that non-Catholic fundamentalists and evangelicals now have an enormous impact on our culture, especially in North America—and so has their rejection of evolution, making Catholics feel they must be suspicious of evolution if they want to be "faithful" in their religion. But there is also something else that has recently come on the scene: the very vocal attacks of atheists who use evolutionary theory as their favorite tool in battling Christian faith. Several of them are influential writers on evolution—biologists such as Richard Dawkins, whose books have sold millions of copies all over the world. Many evangelical Christians easily bought into that clash, attacking *evolution* as the greatest threat to their beliefs—instead of taking on these atheists. As a result of all this, the issue of *evolution* has become highly suspect, even among Catholics. Lost in this debate is the profound Catholic truth, affirmed by popes and theologians from the earliest Church until today, that faith can never conflict with the truths of science—not even evolution.

Being a human geneticist, I have no doubt that we do need to teach our next generation about evolution. Science has given us so much in modern life that we don't want to go back to the time when the earth was considered flat, and we had no scientific accomplishments such as television, phones, medication, or surgery to improve our lives. Still we have a love-hate relationship with science: We want scientists to keep their predictive hands off our lives, yet we want our medical doctors to know what determines what so they can cure us. Perhaps we should teach science with a little more reservation. Science deals only with what can be counted and measured, and therefore has nothing to say about everything else in life, the realm that can't be counted. Besides, science is and remains a fallible enterprise; many scientific statements have been and in time still need to be revised. But at least science keeps learning from its mistakes. Because reason also requires *faith*, this book is one long argument against the arrogance of some narrow-minded scientists.

Being a Catholic, I am very aware that there is more to life than science. Science may be everywhere, but science is certainly not all there is; science is actually a very limited undertaking. And that's where religion, creation, and Adam and Eve come in. Public schools (and even some Catholic schools) want to stay away from such issues, but ignoring them doesn't make those issues go away. But should they become a new science—like creationism and the theory of "intelligent design" would have it? No, they shouldn't, for the simple reason that science has earned its solid reputation the way it is. Yes, there is more to life than science, but because faith also requires *reason*, this book is also one long argument against the tyranny of some fundamentalist believers.

In other words, science should never silence religion, nor should religion ever silence science. So let's not turn science into a pseudo-religion, nor turn religion into a semi-science. Is such a thing possible? Yes, I think it is, as the rest of the book will show in more detail.

In writing this book, I had a wide audience of educated Catholics in mind. Why Catholics? The reason is that I am a dedicated Catholic myself, and Catholicism has a unique blend of faith and reason. But the book is more specifically intended for college students, biology teachers, home schoolers, parents with children in high school or college, clergy, teachers of religious education, parish study groups, and for all those troubled by the seeming contradiction between scientific knowledge and their religious faith. I had also in mind those who feel that science is pulling them away from their faith. I hope and pray that all these people will highly benefit from this book.

Some chapters contain supplementary material at the end, which are rather technical sections providing more in-depth information that some readers may want to leave out, without losing the main line of thought. While this information is informative and enriching, readers can skip these more detailed extras if desired.

For questions and requests, or to schedule a speaking event, please feel free to contact me at *www.where-do-we-come-from.com*.

# CHAPTER I

———⟨◇⟩———

# The Roman Catholic Position

## 1.1 What the Church Teaches About Faith and Reason

The Roman Catholic Church has always stood behind the motto of "Faith *and* Reason," which goes at least as far back as the martyr Saint Justin (103–165). The First Vatican Council condemned the doctrine that faith is irrational; it insisted that faith is always in harmony with reason (but need not be subject to scientific demonstration). Some people think that when we begin to use reason, we have no choice but to abandon faith; conversely, they think that if we have faith, we cannot use reason. The Church teaches differently: discovering the truth through reason can never destroy faith. Pope Benedict XVI has made faith and reason all the more prominent in the Church. In so doing, he continues the tradition of his predecessor, Pope John Paul II, who issued the encyclical *Fides et Ratio* on the relationship between faith and reason. To put the message briefly, Catholics are supposed to be reasonable in their faith, and faithful in their reasoning. Our minds should work in the light of reason as well as in the light of faith.

May we also apply this motto of Faith and Reason to the issue of religion and science? Certainly! The Catholic Church has a longstanding record of honoring both religion (faith) and science (reason). Around 400, Saint Augustine wrote: "It not infrequently happens that something about the earth, about the sky, . . . about the nature of animals, of fruits, of stones, and of other such things, may be known with the greatest certainty by reasoning or by experience, even by one who is not a Christian."[1] But this belief became even more explicit with Saint Albert the Great (or Albertus Magnus, 1206–1280), a scientist and a doctor of the Church. Albert was the teacher of another *doctor of the Church*, Saint Thomas Aquinas. As a scientist, Albert had quite a track record for his time: in addition to his theological works, he discovered the element arsenic; experimented with photosensitive chemicals, including silver nitrate; and made disciplined observations in plant anatomy and animal embryology. In all his works, he advocated the peaceful coexistence of science and religion, advising us to turn to a theologian in matters of faith, but to a physician or scientist in matters of medicine or physics. He explicitly proclaimed that faith and reason can never contradict each other.

Although he did not do experiments as his teacher did, Saint Thomas Aquinas followed in his footsteps. Aquinas may not have put his foot inside the gates of science, but "he certainly pioneered a crucial phase of the march toward those gates."[2] Saint Thomas made it very clear that reason can never arrive at a conclusion opposed to faith, because God himself created the reasoning mind. In saying this, Aquinas cleared the way for science as well.

But before science could become the kind of science we know today, some hurdles remained. A major obstacle was the great impact the ancient Greek philosophers Aristotle and Pythagoras still had through their works—which came down to us through the Christian monks who had laboriously copied them. Aristotle and Pythagoras believed that the world is the way it is because it must be that way; nature is supposed to dance to the tune of those philosophers, for no deity could have created a world in defiance of Aristotelian or Pythagorean philosophy, period! But Christians had started to see the world differently. Two of them in particular, the Franciscans Roger Bacon (c. 1214–1294; not to be confused with the philosopher Francis Bacon) and William of Ockham (c. 1280–1349)—both following in the footsteps of another early scientist, Bishop Robert Grosseteste (1175–1253)—said that we cannot assume that God did

---

1. The Literal Meaning of Genesis, 1:19.

2. Stanley L. Jaki OSB, *The Road of Science and the Ways to God* (Chicago: University of Chicago Press, 1978), 39.

things the way we think he ought to have, since God can do whatever he likes. The person who wants to have dominion over nature must begin by listening, observing, and respecting God's acts in creation. It is only in this way that the astronomer Copernicus could later come up with the daring declaration that nothing was easier for God than to have the earth move, if he so wished.

Therefore, the only way to find out what God has actually done is to go out and look—in other words, to do experiments. Bacon performed and described various experiments (for example, he manufactured gunpowder, worked extensively with lenses, and used a *camera obscura* to observe solar eclipses); understandably, he urged theologians to study all sciences closely, strongly championing experimental study over reliance on authority. In this Catholic view (basically dating back to Saint Augustine), the universe was seen as a law-abiding structure because it had been created by a lawful God. The Book of Genesis teaches us that the universe was created by a rational intellect that is capable of being rationally investigated. This means that the universe is open to analysis by reason, including science, as the universe was created according to the Creator's mind.

Although many may call the Middle Ages the "Dark Ages," they were not dark; if they seem dark, it's more by lack of historical sources than by a void of culture. The Church kept the candle of learning alive in her monasteries and universities. During the Middle Ages the scientific method was born, and science became a formal discipline separate from philosophy. It is because of Church scholars such as the Dominicans Albert the Great and Thomas Aquinas, along with the Franciscans Roger Bacon and William of Ockham and their followers, that the West could carry on the spirit of scientific inquiry, which enabled science to emerge and prosper, and would later give rise to Europe's taking the lead in science.

The popes have confirmed this long-standing tradition in the Catholic Church of advocating the peaceful coexistence of science and religion. Writing more than a hundred years ago, Pope Leo XIII (1878–1903)[3] said:

> There can never, indeed, be any real discrepancy between the theologian and the physicist, as long as each confines himself within his own lines . . .

---

3. The years given for the popes indicate their pontificates. Ed.

If dissension should arise between them . . . we must remember, first, that the sacred writers, or to speak more accurately, the Holy Ghost "Who spoke by them, did not intend to teach men these things (that is to say, the essential nature of the things of the visible universe), things in no way profitable unto salvation" (Saint Augustine, *The Literal Meaning of Genesis*, 2:9, 20). Hence they did not seek to penetrate the secrets of nature, but rather described and dealt with things in more or less figurative language, or in terms which were commonly used at the time, and which in many instances are in daily use at this day, even by the most eminent men of science.[4]

Pope Pius XI (1922–1939) promoted a renewed dialogue between science and religion. In 1936 he reestablished the *Pontifical Academy of Sciences* to support serious scientific study within the Catholic Church. On that occasion, the pontiff said:

Science, when it is real cognition, is never in contrast with the truth of the Christian faith. Indeed, as is well known to those who study the history of science, it must be recognized that the Roman Pontiffs and the Catholic Church have always fostered the research of the learned in the experimental field.[5]

Pope Pius XI gave his last pontifical address at this academy, which focuses on the harmonious relation between science and religion. In it, he quoted from the Book of Wisdom: "you have disposed all things by measure and number and weight" (11:20)—and then the Holy Father continued:

It is like going into an immense laboratory of chemistry, of physics, of astronomy. Few indeed can admire the profound beauty of such words as well as those who make sciences their profession. . . . The created world receives weight, number, and measure through the hands of God. This is true for everything: for the greatest as much as for the smallest. [6]

His successor, Pope Pius XII, continued this Catholic approach. The pontiff categorically stated that "true science discovers God in an ever-increasing degree—as though God were waiting behind every door opened

---

4. Leo XIII, *Providentissimus Deus*, no. 18.

5. Pius XI, *Motu Proprio*, AAS 28, 1936, 427.

6. Pius XI, Address to the Plenary Session of the Academy: "The Complex Subject of Science Is the Reality of the Created Universe," December 18, 1938.

by science."[7] And John Paul II once again emphasized the role and goals of the Academy with these words as "a visible sign, raised amongst the peoples of the world, of the profound harmony that can exist between the truths of science and the truths of faith."[8]

The Catholic Church has no fear of science or scientific discovery, but stands in a long tradition of defending the position that faith and reason—or religion and science, for that matter—do not contradict but rather complement each other as coming from the same source: God. The Church unquestionably acknowledges that God speaks to us in two different ways: That is, through the Book of Scripture as well as through the Book of Nature—both coming from the same source: God.

Standing within this strong and solid tradition, Vatican II declared that "if methodical investigation within every branch of learning is carried out in a genuinely scientific manner and in accord with moral norms, it never truly conflicts with faith, for earthly matters and the concerns of faith derive from the same God."[9]

This view is well put and summarized in the *Catechism of the Catholic Church*:

> [M]ethodical research in all branches of knowledge, provided it is carried out in a truly scientific manner and does not override moral laws, can never conflict with the faith, because the things of the world and the things of the faith derive from the same God. The humble and persevering investigator of the secrets of nature is being led, as it were, by the hand of God in spite of himself, for it is God, the conserver of all things, who made them what they are.[10]

How does all of this relate to the issue of creation and evolution? The *Catechism of the Catholic Church* touches only briefly on the issue of evolution. It says:

> The question about the origins of the world and of man has been the object of many scientific studies that have splendidly enriched our knowledge of the age and dimensions of the cosmos, the development of life-forms and

---

7. Pius XII, Address to the Pontifical Academy of Sciences, November 22, 1951.

8. John Paul II, Address to the Pontifical Academy of Sciences, November 10, 1979.

9. *Gaudium et Spes*, 36.

10. *Catechism of the Catholic Church* (hereafter cited as *CCC*), 2nd ed. (Washington, DC: United States Conference of Catholic Bishops, 2006), no. 159.

the appearance of man. These discoveries invite us to even greater admiration for the greatness of the Creator, prompting us to give him thanks for all his works and for the understanding and wisdom he gives to scholars and researchers.[11]

Again, these insights about the relationship between creation and evolution have a much longer history. Although there had been lesser interventions on the subject of evolution before, in 1950 Pope Pius XII issued the encyclical *Humani Generis*, in which he declared that opinions favorable and unfavorable to evolution must be carefully weighed and judged. He did, however, speak against certain philosophical and evolutionary ideas, particularly some associated with the Jesuit paleontologist Pierre Teilhard de Chardin, who had nearly made evolution into a semireligion by proclaiming the absorption of all humans in an ongoing evolution toward his so-called Omega Point. At the same time, the Holy Father gave the most authoritative statement to that date regarding the possibility of Catholics holding certain versions of evolutionary theory. He wrote:

> The Teaching Authority of the Church does not forbid that—in conformity with the present state of human sciences and sacred theology —research and discussions, on the part of men experienced in both fields, take place with regard to the doctrine of evolution, in as far as it inquires into the origin of the human body as coming from pre-existent and living matter—for the Catholic faith obliges us to hold that souls are immediately created by God. However, this must be done in such a way that the reasons for both opinions, that is, those favorable and those unfavorable to evolution, be weighed and judged with the necessary seriousness, moderation, and measure, and provided that all are prepared to submit to the judgment of the Church, to whom Christ has given the mission of interpreting authentically the Sacred Scriptures and of defending the dogmas of faith.[12]

In April 1985, Pope John Paul II addressed a symposium on evolution:

> Rightly comprehended, faith in creation or a correctly understood teaching of evolution does not create obstacles: Evolution in fact presupposes creation; creation situates itself in the light of evolution as an event which extends itself through time—as a continual creation—in which God becomes visible to the eyes of the believers as "Creator of heaven and earth."[13]

---

11. Ibid., no. 283.

12. Pius XII, *Humani Generis*, no. 36.

13. Address to a symposion on evolution, April 1985.

Several months later, the same pope declared during a general audience:

All the observations concerning the development of life lead to a similar conclusion. The evolution of living beings, of which science seeks to determine the stages and to discern the mechanism, presents an internal finality which arouses admiration. This finality, which directs beings in a direction for which they are not responsible or in charge, obliges one to suppose a Mind which is its Inventor, its Creator.[14]

The following year, the Holy Father reiterated his view regarding the relationship between creation and evolution:

... from the viewpoint of the doctrine of the faith, there are no difficulties in explaining the origin of man in regard to the body, by means of the theory of evolution. But it must be added that this hypothesis proposes only a probability, not a scientific certainty.

However, the doctrine of faith invariably affirms that man's spiritual soul is created directly by God. According to the hypothesis mentioned, it is possible that the human body, following the order impressed by the Creator on the energies of life, could have been gradually prepared in the forms of antecedent living beings. However, the human soul, on which man's humanity definitively depends, cannot emerge from matter, since the soul is of a spiritual nature.[15]

Then, in 1996, John Paul II addressed the subject of evolution again. The general tone of the address was positive but cautious. He said positive things about science but also stressed the limits of science in regard to human origins. In addition, he discussed various interpretations of human evolution that are incompatible with the Catholic faith. He explained that materialistic, reductionistic, and spiritualistic versions of evolutionary theory cannot be reconciled with Christianity. These are philosophies, he noted, not science. As such, they are subject to philosophical refutation. The final judgment regarding their truth or falsity belongs to philosophy and, in a certain way, to theology. But regarding the scientific part of evolution, he said:

Today, almost half a century after the publication of the encyclical [*Humani Generis*, 1950], some new findings lead us toward the recognition of evolution as more than a hypothesis. It is indeed remarkable that this theory has been progressively accepted by researchers, following a series of discoveries in various fields of knowledge. The convergence in

---

14. John Paul II, general audience, July 10, 1985.

15. John Paul II, general audiences, January 29 and April 16, 1986.

the results of these independent studies—which was neither planned nor sought—is in itself a significant argument in favor of this theory.[16]

In the fall of 2004, the International Theological Commission (ITC, a Pontifical Commission in the Vatican) touched on issues of creation and evolution:

> Since it has been demonstrated that all living organisms on earth are genetically related, it is virtually certain that all living organisms have descended from this first organism. Converging evidence from many studies in the physical and biological sciences furnishes mounting support for some theory of evolution to account for the development and diversification of life on earth, while controversy continues over the pace and mechanisms of evolution.[17]

In other words, exactly *how* and *how fast* evolution occurred remain controversial issues, but *that* evolution happened the commission seems to accept.

In 1995, then-Cardinal Joseph Ratzinger published a series of homilies on creation. He argued there that we shouldn't speak of "creation or evolution," but of "creation *and* evolution" (emphasis added). He also referred to what he called "the inner unity of creation and evolution, and faith and reason."[18] During his pontificate, Benedict XVI has—like his predecessor—consistently opposed the misguided notion that evolution somehow proves there is no God who created us in love. In his first homily as pontiff, in 2005, he insisted: "We are not some casual and meaningless product of evolution. Each of us is the result of a thought of God. Each of us is willed, each of us is loved, each of us is necessary."[19]

On July 26, 2007 Pope Benedict XVI was more specific; he said to 400 priests at a two-hour event that he is puzzled by the current debate in the United States and his native Germany over creationism and evolution. He told them that debaters wrongly present the two sides

> as if they were alternatives that are exclusive—whoever believes in the creator could not believe in evolution, and whoever asserts belief in evolution would have to disbelieve in God. . . . This contrast is an absurdity, because

---

16. John Paul II, Address to the Pontifical Academy of Sciences, October 22, 1996.

17. International Theological Commission, *Communion and Stewardship: Human Persons Created in the Image of God*, 2004, no. 63.

18. Joseph Ratzinger, In the Beginning, trans. Boniface Ramsey (Grand Rapids: Eerdmans, 1995).

19. Benedict XVI, Homily at the Mass for the inauguration of his pontificate, April 24, 2005.

there are many scientific tests in favor of evolution, which appears as a reality that we must see and [which] enriches our understanding of life and being. But the doctrine of evolution does not answer all questions, and it does not answer above all the great philosophical question: From where does everything come? [20]

In conclusion, the popes of the past century have had little trouble in aligning their teaching with evolutionary theory, and Catholic theologians from Cardinal John Henry Newman to Cardinal Avery Dulles easily equated their religious faith and biblical scholarship with the advance in evidence for evolution.

So why do many Catholics still feel uncomfortable with the issue of evolution? Not so long ago, many Catholics in the pews understood that evolution was somehow consistent with Church teaching. What has changed is not Church teaching, or evolutionary theory, but the fact that non-Catholic fundamentalists and evangelicals now have an enormous impact on our culture, as has their rejection of evolution, making Catholics feel they must be suspicious of evolution if they want to be faithful to their religion. But something else has also changed recently: the appearance of atheists who use evolutionary theory as their favorite tool in battling Christian faith. Some of them are influential writers on evolution —biologists such as Richard Dawkins, whose books, in which he declares a war against religion, have sold millions of copies.

Many evangelical Christians responded by attacking *evolution* (instead of the ideology of those atheists) as the greatest threat to their beliefs. So the issue of evolution has become highly suspect, even with Catholics—no matter what Roman pontiffs and prominent Church theologians and cardinals have said to the contrary.

Some Catholics may still think that evolution is not compatible with Catholic teaching. Yet, whether evolution occurred or not is an issue for the biological sciences to determine; and they have done so, as we will see later on in this book. But we can also conclude that these pontiffs and theologians deem at least some forms of evolutionary theory to be compatible with the Catholic faith. If one rejects evolution altogether—not just some philosophically erroneous versions of it—one must do so on grounds other than incompatibility with Christianity. So we should be

---

20. Benedict XVI, meeting with the clergy.

cautious in rejecting evolution, for Saint Augustine once warned us that it is "dangerous to have an infidel hear a Christian ... talking nonsense."[21] One would indeed need very strong reasons to dissent as a Christian or Catholic.

For that reason, I would suggest we look in the Book of Scripture as well as in the Book of Nature for an answer to the life-size question: Where do we come from?

<hr>

## DELVING DEEPER

### What About the Galileo Conflict?

Perhaps you have reservations about whether the Church has always been "reasonable" in honoring faith and reason. What about the conflict between Galileo and the Church? Was it a reasonable debate? Yes, it probably was—more so than some might like to hear. True, some theologians at the time did base their attacks against Galileo on a few lines in the Bible, translated poorly, taken literally, interpreted wrongly, and/or taken out of context—in texts such as Psalms 93:1 and 104:5, which say that God created the earth so it can never be "moved." The Hebrew word used here means "to falter, shake, wobble, slip, or slide"; so perhaps "shaken" would be a better translation than "moved." The core message here is that God is the Creator of this world, so nothing really terrifying or earth-shaking can ever happen to his creation, because we are in good hands. Those theologians should have been more cautious.

The problem in the Galileo conflict was not about a "flat earth." Pythagoras and others had already assumed that the earth was a sphere. Although Saint Basil the Great declared it a matter of no interest to us whether the earth is a sphere or a cylinder or a disk or concave in the middle like a fan, influential Christian thinkers such as Saint Clement, Origen, Saint Ambrose, Saint Augustine, and Saint Thomas Aquinas all accepted that the earth was a globe.[22]

<hr>

21. The Literal Meaning of Genesis, 1:20.

22. For a good analysis of this issue, see James Hannam, *God's Philosophers: How the Medieval World Laid the Foundations of Modern Science* (London: Icon Books, 2010).

A more serious problem, however, was the heliocentric model (with the sun in the center) versus the old geocentric model (with the earth in the center). Copernicus was the first to publish the idea of a heliocentric model in 1543, suggesting that the earth orbited the sun. But because, like Ptolemy (c. A.D. 90–168), he insisted on circular orbits, his heliocentric model was no more accurate than Ptolemy's geocentric one. Johannes Kepler improved the model by using the Copernican system but adding elliptical orbits. As his writings make clear, Kepler had been inspired by his faith to figure out a perfect system, because he knew God would not tolerate the inaccuracies that plagued the other models. Yet, Kepler was persecuted by the Protestant Faculty at Tübingen and took refuge with the Jesuits in 1596. Martin Luther dismissed Copernicus as "that fool," and the theologian Phillip Melancthon condemned Copernicanism as "dishonest" and "pernicious."

Then Galileo entered the scene. In 1632, he published, with papal permission, a book called *Dialogue Concerning the Two Chief World Systems.* In it, he supported Copernicus rather than Kepler, so Galileo's heliocentric model was also not any better than Ptolemy's geocentric one. In addition, he ran into trouble because of a perceived insult concerning the Pope in his book. When tried by the Holy Office, Galileo refused to adopt Kepler's system, because his Pythagorean philosophy forced him to stick with "perfect" circles rather than "imperfect" ellipses (making him advocate circular motions of a spherical earth)—so he lost even the scientific argument. In addition, he argued that the tides were a direct consequence of the earth's motion—which is inconsistent even with his own principles of dynamics. From then on, it went downhill. Galileo was forced to renounce his opinions, but refused to do so, and so was confined to his home for the rest of his life. Pope John Paul II speaks of a "Tragic mutual incomprehension."[23] This part of Church history is certainly not one of the best—a human drama played out by a cast of flawed and finite characters on both sides.

Under the surface, though, much more was going on in this debate. Many Jesuit astronomers actually agreed with the new astronomy. On his own account, Galileo regarded the Jesuits of the Roman College, the leading astronomers of the day, as modern-minded humanists, friends of

---

23. Speech on October 1, 1992, to the Pontifical Academy of Sciences.

science and discovery. [24] The Jesuits actually had better telescopes than he did, so Galileo was happy to receive one of theirs as a gift. In time, however, he would lose their support because of a dispute over comets with the Jesuit mathematician-astronomer Fr. Horatio Grassi (who would eventually turn out to be right). The frequency and acidity of Galileo's attacks played an important role in causing many Jesuits to withdraw their support of Galileo—which he later would need so badly. What irked Church officials was not so much what Galileo was saying, but how he was saying it.

Like the Jesuit astronomers, many theologians at the time were "modern-minded." One of the main players in the debate was Saint Robert Bellarmine, a Jesuit cardinal. He distinguished two types of astronomy:[25] On the one hand, he recognized a mathematical astronomy that tries to come up with systems that do justice to astronomical phenomena. On the other hand, he singled out a physical astronomy that seeks to ascertain which mathematical systems actually apply to the physical structure of the heavens. The cardinal's reasoning was logical and perfectly correct: the same set of facts may be consistent with different (mathematical) theories, so we need to figure out which theory is true. Bellarmine deemed it harmless to claim that the sun is in the center if one uses a mathematical approach. But such a claim, he said, would require much more evidence, if one were to claim this to actually be the case in a physical sense. He wrote, "if there were a true demonstration that . . . the sun did not go around the earth but the earth went around the sun, then it would be necessary to use careful consideration in explaining the Scriptures that seemed contrary."[26] All he required was stronger scientific evidence.

Indeed, the scientific case was not as clear as some think. If we use Aristotelian theories of impulse and relative motion, the theory advanced by Copernicus, as well as by Galileo, appears to be falsified by the fact that objects fall vertically on earth rather than diagonally (the famous so-called tower argument). Additional facts seemed to confirm that the earth did not move, for if it did, the clouds would be left behind (as Galileo himself

24. See William Wallace, *Galileo and His Sources* (Princeton University Press, 1984). See also Arthur Koestler, "The Greatest Scandal in Christendom," *The Observer,* London, February 2, 1964, 21.

25. E.g. in his letter of April 12, 1615, to Fr. Foscarini—as a reaction to Galileo's "Letter to Christina."

26. In his letter to Fr. Foscarini.

had remarked in a lecture of 1601). As the late University of California at Berkeley philosopher of science Paul Feyerabend pointed out, one could even state that Galileo's opponents kept closer to reason than Galileo himself.[27] Galileo actually introduced theories that are inconsistent with well-established facts. The observation that objects fall vertically on earth required a new interpretation to make it compatible with Copernican theory. Galileo was able to make such a change about the nature of impulse and relative motion, but before such theories were articulated, he had to use ad hoc methods and proceed counter-inductively—in defiance of reason, given the knowledge available at the time. He even had to reluctantly admit that his mentor Copernicus had committed what Galileo called "a rape of the senses."

In reality, there was a battle going on behind the scientific scenes: the power of formal sciences such as mathematics versus the power of empirical sciences—the latter depending on observational tools such as telescopes (and microscopes), which must first prove their reliability. Like students who use a microscope for the first time and see hardly anything, astronomers must learn to use telescopes. When Galileo demonstrated his simple telescope to twenty-five professors in Bologna (1610), all admitted the instrument seemed to deceive; some fixed stars were actually seen double. Even Galileo conceded in a letter to Kepler that many people were unable to see what they were "supposed" to see through his telescope. Ironically, Galileo would refer to comets as "optical illusions," when he thought it would suit him well during his dispute about comets with Fr. Grassi.

We must also realize that no good optical theory was available to explain the working of telescopes until the work of René Descartes, Isaac Newton, and Christiaan Huygens (after 1650). So understandably, many scientists thought that all the things the new telescope showed them could only be artifacts or optical illusions. A tube that only shows what cannot exist would not be a very reliable tube, right? Again, the debate seems basically reasonable, no matter how awful the final outcome concerning Galileo may appear.

Yet, we should also acknowledge that the Church has learned from this experience. Undoubtedly, the Church at the time could and should have

---

27. Paul Feyerabend, *Against Method: Outline of an Anarchistic Theory of Knowledge* (New York: Verso Books, 1975), ch. 13.

listened more intently to its doctors of the Church, dedicated advocates for a peaceful coexistence of science and religion. Pope Pius XII called Galileo one of the "most audacious heroes of research . . . not afraid of the stumbling blocks and the risks on the way."[28] And in 1983, Pope John Paul II said that the Galileo case had led the Church "to a more mature attitude and a more accurate grasp of the authority proper to her," enabling her better to dis-tinguish between "essentials of the faith" and the "scientific systems of a given age."[29] Perhaps Saint Albert's promotion of a peaceful coexistence of science and religion should have been taken more seriously much sooner.

---

28. Pius XII, Address to the Pontifical Academy of Sciences, 1939.

29. John Paul II, *Address to an International Symposium on the Occasion of the 350th Anniversary of the Publication of Galileo's Dialogue Concerning the Two Chief World Systems*, May 9, 1983.

# CHAPTER 2

———◦❈◦———

# Where We Come From—
# According to the Bible

## 2.1 Two Creation Accounts

The Bible has *two* different accounts of creation—the first in Genesis 1:1–2:4a, and the second in Genesis 2:4b–25. Stretching the imagination a bit, we could even find a third creation account in the Book of Job, starting in chapter 38, when God interrogates Job, saying, "Where were you when I laid the foundation of the earth?" And then God goes into all the elements of nature that he created—which is done in an alternation of "Who has. . . ?" and "Have you . . . ?" In the process, Job's stature grows smaller and smaller. And Psalm 104 praises God's creation: "O Lord, how manifold are your works! In wisdom you have made them all. . . . When you send forth your spirit, they are created; and you renew the face of the earth." Doesn't that sound like creation in the making, or creation in action? Somehow the Bible is telling us there are many ways of looking at creation.

Let's begin with a brief summary of Genesis 1. It relates a clear message: "In the beginning, God created the heavens and the earth." From the first two verses, however, it isn't clear whether God created space and time out of nothing (as verse 1 suggests) or out of the chaos of primordial waters (as verse 2 suggests, with the Spirit of God hovering over the waters). The

Catholic teaching speaks of creation out of nothing (*ex nihilo*[1]) and takes verse 2 as the next step.

The rest of Genesis 1 repeats: "God said," "God called," "God saw that it was good, very good." This repetitive structure can also be found in the Book of Job: "Who has ...? ... Have you ...?" According to both accounts, it is God who has done all of this—not a deity, but the God of the Covenant, our God. It is obvious in every sentence that not only did he want us, but also that he had plans for us and for our world. The goodness of creation is a clear sign of God's love.

In Genesis 1, all God's work of creation is done in one good and holy week: The light rises, the morning dawns, the water recedes, the earth emerges, and plants start to grow and blossom. The clouds disappear and the sun shines. Fish, birds, and land animals appear. Finally a human being comes on stage, taking possession of the land as a steward or trustee. Let us see how everything develops daily during that special week of creation:

### The first day

God summons the light—even before the sun rises on the fourth day. Apparently, the real light does not come from the sun, but finds its origin in God's word. As long as God keeps speaking (creating), it will never become dark again. Night is not darkness, only a time of rest.

### The second day

God separates the waters above and below, sets up a firmament to divide them. This is the only day we don't hear the phrase "It was good." Did the writer forget? I don't think so. As it turns out, it wasn't completely good yet. Although the water was brought under control, it could still break out and menace people, as we all know from floods, tsunamis, and the like. It won't be until the very end of the Bible that we hear this sigh of relief: "and the sea was no more" (Rev 21:1).

### The third day

We see land, a big garden, and grounds for a good life. No wonder the text mentions twice that everything is good, for it is heading to the Promised Land. Isn't that good news?

---

1. See *CCC*, no. 296.

### The fourth day

Now it is time for the creation of "lamps." Those lamps are not called by their own names—sun, moon, stars—for these were popular names of gods at the time. People had gotten used to believing in their occult powers of determining a person's character, fate, destiny. But no, Genesis says, they are merely lamps that give light to live and work by.

### The fifth day

Fish and birds come alive. Genesis mentions them because Israel's neighboring peoples worshiped fish and birds. Egypt, for example, adored sacred pigeons, eagles, falcons, and other bird-headed gods. According to Genesis, God is in control of all those beasts. They are mere creatures, definitely not deities.

### The sixth day

On this tremendously busy day, God creates the land animals. Genesis repeats the phrase, "according to their kinds." In other words, don't mix them up; some kinds are clean and kosher, but others are not. Never idolize them as the neighboring peoples worship sacred cows, cats, rams, lions, serpents, and golden calves. Then, at last, a human being appears. Were human beings also created according to their kind? No, they were *not*, for there are no different "kinds" of humanity: no black and white, no healthy and disabled, no supremacists and misfits, no rich and poor, no high and low, no good and bad—and most of all, no mortal people (like you and me) versus divine people (such as pharaohs and kings). Only one kind of humanity exists: the very kind God created in his own image and likeness.

### The seventh day

This is the last day of the week, in line with Israel's rhythm of living and working. Notice that God completes his work of creation only on the seventh day. Creation isn't complete until the Sabbath has been created—a day of rest, a feast day. Humans do not live to work, but they work in order to live—or in Jesus' words, "The Sabbath was made for humankind, and not humankind for the Sabbath" (Mk 2:27). The seventh day is part of

God's creation—actually, the very purpose of his creation. That is why this day has no ending; it is an endless day, as creation is not something that ended long ago. It is also a day of celebration: because God glorified all human beings, so in turn they should glorify their Creator all their lives, in particular on the Day of the Lord every single week.

What happens after this stunning creation account? New questions surface, such as: Is everything really that rosy? Just look around! Isn't there more to the story? Why did God's good intentions seem to have turned around? This is where the *second* creation account comes in, but this time without any talk of creation "days."

It is almost as if the Bible starts all over again, but with roles reversed. Whereas Genesis 1 paints an immense world with abundant water, carrying a tiny human being who appears at the eleventh hour while everything is waiting for him, Genesis 2 describes a mirror image: a tiny world with a shortage of water, in which a human being stalks about like a giant and nothing starts working until this being is around. In Genesis 2, everything is on hold until humankind arrives; all the earth hungers and thirsts until a human being begins to cultivate it; the animals do not have names until this human being gives them names. Picture this *Adam* (which is Hebrew for man, human being) standing on the *adama* (Hebrew for ground or field); and it happens to be the clay taken from this very *adama* of which *Adam* was made. But suddenly things change. Once humanity is around, but neglects its calling, creation turns sour.

Genesis 2 teaches three things about humanity. First, it shows us *what* we are. It tells us that God first molds the mud, and then blows his own breath into it. Not only are we made of mud, but we actually are mud or dust. We are and will always be a piece of mud muddling on. As we hear on each Ash Wednesday, "You are dust, and to dust you will return." But we are also more: a living soul—only thanks to God's breath. God created us as a composite of body and soul. Second, Genesis 2 describes *where* we are. We are in a garden, a piece of land, good soil—not a fairy-tale paradise. If we spoil the soil, we destroy the garden. Third, Genesis 2 tells us *why* we are there. God put us in the garden to "till it and keep it." The Hebrew puts it in a more striking way: "to serve and to keep watch over." Therefore, we are merely servants, shepherds, stewards, trustees. And that's where that famous tree comes in. In Israel, every garden was supposed to have one such tree—the owner's tree. By respecting another's tree, you acknowledge that you are not its owner but its steward, just number two. Once humans act like the owner, like number one, creation immediately turns sour.

Then Genesis 2 states that it is not good for creation for the man to be alone. This is the first time the Bible states that something is *not* good. But notice the exact wording. It's not that it wouldn't be good for *man* to be alone; no, it is not good for *creation* that man is alone. Creation will not come to its destination until man is no longer alone, no longer one-sided, but rather man and wo-man, male and fe-male. Yet, no other creature could ever qualify as a real human companion.

So God put Adam in a deep sleep, actually a death-sleep, so the lonely and one-sided person dies. Then God "took one of his sides"—one of those so-called ribs. (The preferred translation of the Hebrew word *tsela* is "side," not "rib"). God split the man and made his two sides into two human beings. From now on, humanity is dual as male and female, but man and woman share the same nature. Each one now has another person to love. "Then the man said, . . . 'this one shall be called Woman, for out of Man this one was taken'" (Gen 2:23). The text here plays on the similar-sounding Hebrew words *ishsha* ("woman") and *ishah* ("her man, her husband").

## 2.2 What the Bible Doesn't Say

A fundamentalist approach to Genesis asserts that the Bible says what it says—in other words, everything in the Bible is a literal, historical, or even scientific account. Our popes teach us a different approach: The Bible sometimes does *not* say what it literally says—or reversed, the Bible sometimes says what it doesn't literally say. In other words, the Bible may have many layers or levels of interpretation.

For example, consider how Jesus speaks in parables. Who is the Prodigal Son, for instance? Is he a concrete historical figure? Or does he stand for the Jews who had wandered away from the strict rules of the Pharisees? Or does he represent the Gentiles who had left their religious cradle long ago? Or is he just you and me, who constantly wander off? The answer is: all of the above.

But the Bible not only speaks at multiple levels, it also comes in multiple forms. A newspaper, for example, contains factual accounts and reports, but also editorial comments, op-eds, and advertisements. We don't read an editorial in the way we read a factual report. We do not read all sections of a newspaper in the same manner.

Similarly, the Bible has many literal, historical reports based on eyewitnesses (*Acts*), but it also has prayers (*Psalms*), reflections (*Ecclesiastes*), fiction (*Esther*), poetry (*Song of Songs*), apocalyptic texts (*Daniel*), visions (*Revelation*), debates (*Job*), parables (found in all Gospels), and letters (Paul's, Peter's). Not all of these elements can be read in the same way. A parable, for example, is not a literal report of a historical event. As Vatican II puts it, "truth is proposed and expressed in a variety of ways, depending on whether its form is that of prophecy, poetry, or some other type of speech."[2]

So how should we understand the two creation accounts in Genesis? They certainly are not eyewitness reports. Pope Pius XII warned us, "What is the literal sense of a passage is not always as obvious in the speeches and writings of the ancient authors of the East, as it is in the works of our own time."[3] Michelangelo certainly knew how to read Genesis when he so awesomely depicted the creation of man on the ceiling of the Sistine Chapel.

There are other indications that we have two different accounts here. Genesis 1 consistently addresses God as "God" (*Elohim*), whereas Genesis 2 refers to him as the "lord God" (*Yahweh Adonai*). Biblical scholars say that Genesis 1 was written by a priestly, so-called *Elohist* writer (probably living in a sedentary setting), whereas Genesis 2 is the product of an earlier, so-called *Yahwist* writer (with a more nomadic background, like Abraham). The text reflects their different styles of writing and thinking. The Yahwist writer, for example, talks in a more down-to-earth manner about God and his actions.

Despite their differences, both authors wrote these accounts under divine inspiration. To put it in more theological terms, Genesis 1 stresses God's *transcendence*—his being far above all we know, while Genesis 2 emphasizes God's *immanence*—his being closely and intimately involved with his creatures. Jews and Christians always try to carefully balance transcendence and immanence, so God doesn't become either too human

---

2. *Dei Verbum*, no. 12.

3. *Divino Afflante Spiritu*, no. 35.

(resembling deities such as Jupiter) or too distant (like the emotionless watchmaker of deism). In its Scriptures, Israel tries to keep both features in balance. On the one hand, God talks to Moses "face to face, as one speaks to a friend" (Ex 33:11). On the other hand, Moses is only allowed to see God's back, for God's "face shall not be seen" (Ex 33:23). God's closeness and God's loftiness are two sides of the same coin. Whoever denies one of these two sides detracts from the biblical message. The Holy Spirit keeps them in a delicate balance. God is part of everything (that's his immanence) without being a physical part of it (that's his transcendence).

In summary, we cannot read Genesis 1 and 2 as a modern, scientific report. It is not so much a literal eyewitness report of *how* God made all things as it is a resounding message *that* God made all things, and that all he made is good since it comes from him—humanity in particular. Genesis teaches a theological, not a scientific message. To read the creation accounts as some kind of science or history is like trying to read Jesus's parables as actual historical events. Reading Genesis this way would inevitably lead us to silly questions such as: "Did Adam and Eve have a belly button?"

The beginning of Genesis is more about the "basics" of creation than the "details" of creation. It is more like a religious creed than a scientific, historical report. So we cannot expect our present-day scientific questions to be answered through the Book of Genesis. For example, chapter 4 of Genesis speaks of Adam and Eve having a son, Cain, then unexpectedly mentions Cain's wife. Where did she come from? Then Adam had another son, Seth, who in turn married a woman coming "from nowhere." Obviously, the beginning of humanity is quite hazy for modern eyes if we go by the Bible—for the simple reason that the Bible is not interested in *scientific* pedigrees. Genesis has a *theological* message. Its main concern is our salvation. Pope Leo XIII expressed the same thought when he said, "the sacred writers . . . did not wish to teach men such truths [as the inner structure of visible objects], which do not help anyone to salvation."[4]

The *Catechism* puts this in perspective when it says "It is not only a question of knowing when and how the universe arose physically, or when man appeared, but rather of discovering the meaning of such an origin: Is the universe governed by chance, blind fate, anonymous necessity, or by a

---

4. Leo XIII, *Providentissimus Deus*, no. 18.

transcendent, intelligent and good being called 'God'?"[5] The answer to this profound question is conveyed even more clearly by Psalm 104. These creation accounts teach the resounding message that the *order* of God's creation frees the world from the caprice of whimsical deities and chaotic powers.

## 2.3 How to Read Creation Accounts

So how we may interpret the first chapters of Genesis? First, we can recall what Pope Benedict XV wrote in 1920: "the Bible, composed by men inspired of the Holy Ghost, has God himself as its principal author, the individual authors constituted as his live instruments. Their activity, however, ought not to be described as automatic writing."[6] That's why Pope Leo XIII said they wrote "in a somewhat figurative language or as the common manner of speech of those times required."[7] The Church proclaims that the Bible was written by *human* authors, yet guided by *divine* inspiration.

Genesis 1 can be read in two ways: a *chronological* reading versus a *structural* reading. According to the *chronological* reading, the six days of creation followed one another in strict chronological order. This view is often coupled with the claim that the six days were standard 24-hour days. Hence, creation would be a process of seven consecutive days constituting the first week of the first month in the first year of the world's calendar.

Some have denied that these seven days were standard days because the Hebrew word used in the text for "day" (*yom*) can mean a longer-than-24-hour period (as it does in Genesis 2:4). But one could counter that Genesis 1 does present the days to us as standard days, for at the end of each day we find a formula like "And there was evening and there was morning, one day."

So it seems that Genesis does present these creation days to us as 24-hour solar days. Should we take this literally? For several reasons I will later develop we can say no, but I would like to mention one thing now. It is peculiar that Genesis 1 uses a timescale (the cycle of day and night) to

---

5. *CCC*, no. 284.

6. Benedict XV, *Spiritus Paraclitus*.

7. *Providentissimus Deus*, 18.

report how that timescale came into being on day one. In a *chronological* version of creation, God needs time (days) in order for him to create everything, so he must first create time itself (on day one). Yet this is odd when seen from a logical viewpoint, for time cannot be created at a "time" when time does not yet exist. In other words, creation cannot follow a timeline, for time itself is a product of creation. Creation creates chronology, but it cannot become part of chronology, nor can chronology be the framework of creation. These considerations are troublesome for a *chronological* interpretation of Genesis 1.

Other indications tell us that we are not dealing with a chronological order: the creation of the sun happens three days after the day/night cycle is established. Origen (c. 185–254), one of the early Fathers of the Church, noticed this problem: "What man of intelligence will believe that the first and the second and third day and the evening and the morning existed without the sun and moon and stars?"[8] In addition, the plants were created one day before the sun was created. This is especially troublesome if a creation "day" is interpreted as a long period of time, since plants need sunlight.

So we can draw the provisional conclusion that Genesis 1 is not meant to be understood as a literal *chronological* account. As Pope Pius XII wrote: ". . . the ancient peoples of the East, in order to express their ideas, did not always employ those forms or kinds of speech which we use today; but rather those used by the men of their times and countries. What those exactly were, the commentator cannot determine as it were in advance, but only after a careful examination of the ancient literature of the East."[9]

This leads to the second possibility—that Genesis 1 is to be given a nonchronological, *structural* reading. Advocates of this view point out that ancient literature commonly placed historical material in a sequential order according to a particular structure or framework, rather than in strict chronological order. The *Catechism* explains that "Scripture presents the work of the Creator symbolically as a succession of six days of divine 'work,' concluded by the 'rest' of the seventh day."[10] Genesis 1 has a *theological*

---

8. *De Principiis.*

9. *Divino Afflante Spiritu*, 36.

10. *CCC*, no. 337.

message. As Saint Augustine says, "it was not the intention of the Spirit of God, who spoke through [the authors of Genesis], to teach men anything that would not be of use to them for their salvation."[11]

The structural interpretation holds that the seven days of creation are not to be taken literally as a chronology of how God made the world. Instead, the structural interpretation stresses that Genesis 1 tells us *what* God did, without attempting to tell us in a literal fashion *when* and *how* God did it. Therefore, the *facts* of creation have been fitted into the structure of a single Hebrew week (the week didn't exist in earlier ancient cultures).

The structural approach is not a new idea. For many centuries, it has been recognized that the six days of creation are divided into two sets of three.

- ❖ In the first set, God divides one thing from another: on day one, he divides the light and the darkness (thus giving rise to day and night); on day two, he divides the waters above from the waters below (thus giving rise to the sky and the sea); and on day three, he divides the waters below from each other (thus giving rise to the dry land). Classically, this section is known as the *work of division*.

- ❖ In the second set of three days, God goes back over the realms that he produced by division in the first three days and then populates or "adorns" them. On day four, he adorns the day and the night with the sun, moon, and stars. On day five, he populates the sky and sea with birds and fish. And on day six, he populates the land (between the divided waters) with the animals and humankind. Classically, this is known as the *work of adornment*.

That this twofold process most likely represents the ordering principle of Genesis 1 is also indicated at the beginning and end of the account. At the beginning, we are told that "the earth was a formless void" (Gen 1:2). The work of *division* cures the "formless" problem, whereas the work of *adornment* fixes the "void" problem. Likewise, at the end of the account we are told "the heavens and the earth were finished [i.e., by *division*], and all their multitude [i.e., by *adornment*]" (2:1). Scholars have recognized for centuries that these ordering principles are at work in Genesis 1. So this is

---

11. *The Literal Meaning of Genesis*, 2:9.

not something modern Bible scholars have come up with—we find this idea, for instance, in the writings of Saint Thomas Aquinas.[12]

We could also give this discussion a more philosophical twist that makes the *structural* reading of Genesis much more sensible than its *chronological* alternative. As said earlier, from a philosophical point of view, it is very hard to interpret creation as a step-by-step process unfolding in a temporal order, for "creation at the beginning of time" is impossible, since there is no time until time has been created. Creating time "at a certain time" is tough to do! In other words, creation is not an event in time, because time is something that, in and of itself, would also require creation. Our world seems to have a beginning and a timeline, but creation itself doesn't have a beginning or a timeline; creation actually makes the beginning of this world and its timeline possible. Consequently, it is hard to take the creation account as a *chronological* description of the initial stages of this world, for without creation, there wouldn't be any world at all. Therefore, creation may create chronology, but it cannot become part of chronology, nor can chronology be the framework of creation. In other words, creation is not exclusively focused on the *beginning* of this world, but on the *origin* of this world; creation is both giving a beginning to all that exists and sustaining in being all that exists. Think of the following analogy: Authors writing a book create the entire book, not just the first page.

Creation essentially means that everything that exists depends on God for its existence. Creation tells us where this world comes from and how it can exist at all. If this interpretation is right, the first words of Genesis— "In the beginning"—do not refer to a trigger event at the beginning of time (something like a Big Bang), because creation must come first before any events (including a Big Bang) can follow. "*In* the beginning" should not be understood in a temporal, chronological, or sequential sense, but rather in a transcending sense—that is, more in the sense of "originally" (*before* any beginning) than "initially" (*at* the beginning). Everything that exists depends on God; he created everything; he is the origin and "beginning" of all there is. When Saint John says, "In the beginning was the Word" (Jn 1:1), he is not speaking of the beginning of all things, as one of the first things to be created, but "before" the beginning of all created things, "before" time existed.

---

12. Cf. *Summa Theologica*, I:74:1.

Upon studying this *structural* interpretation a bit further, we could even detect what has been called the "polemic design" of the first creation account: Genesis 1 is a radical and sweeping affirmation of monotheism vis-à-vis polytheism, syncretism, and idolatry.[13] Most of the peoples surrounding Israel regarded the various regions of nature as actually *divine*: they worshiped the sun, moon, and stars as gods; they had sky gods; earth gods; water gods; gods of light and darkness, rivers and vegetation, animals and fertility. Look again at the structure of Genesis 1 to see this point:

❖ light and darkness (day one) are populated by the greater and lesser lights (day four);

❖ firmament and waters (day two) are populated by birds and fish (day five);

❖ earth and vegetation (day three) are populated by animals and humans (day six).

Through this structure Genesis 1 proclaims its radical and imperative affirmation of monotheism. Each day dismisses an additional cluster of deities: On the first day, the gods of light and darkness; on the second day, the gods of sky and sea; on the third day, earth gods and gods of vegetation; on the fourth day, sun, moon, and star gods (including astrology); on the fifth and sixth days, gods from the animal kingdom (such as sacred falcons, lions, serpents, and golden calves). Finally, even humans are emptied of any *intrinsic* divinity, even while they are *granted* a divine likeness (yes, all of them, from the greatest to the least, and not just pharaohs, kings, and heroes). So each day of creation shows us another set of idols being smashed. Nothing on earth is god, but everything comes from God. Obviously, the issue at stake in Genesis 1 is idolatry, not science; mythology, not natural history; theology, not chronology; theo-logy, not sciento-logy. Genesis proclaims monotheism, not a scientific theory of origin. It concludes that creation is *good*, very good, but it is certainly not *divine*. God is the creator of everything, and there are no other gods beside him.

Another point indicates that we should read Genesis 1 as a structured polemic against idolatry. The final verse (2:4a) concludes: "These are the generations of the heavens and the earth when they were created." If this

---

13. See, for instance, the work of theologian Conrad Hyers, especially his "Biblical Literalism: Constricting the Cosmic Dance" in *Is God a Creationist?*, ed. R. M. Frye (New York: Scribner, 1982).

truly were a chronology of creation days, why would it use the word *genera-tions* (for that's what *toledoth* in Hebrew means). The answer is clear now. If we were to ask how all these pagan deities were related to one another in the pantheons of the day, the most common answer would have been that they were all members of the same family tree. But in opposition to all these pagan pantheons with their divine pedigrees and genealogies, Genesis 1 proclaims that each of them was created by the only living God: "These are the *generations* of the heavens and the earth when they were *created*." Genesis thus dismisses all the divine genealogies and family trees.

By smashing all idols, the writer of Genesis 1 obeys the words God spoke at Horeb: "Take care and watch yourselves closely, so that you do not act corruptly by making an idol for yourselves, in the form of any figure— the likeness of male or female, the likeness of any animal that is on the earth, the likeness of any winged bird that flies in the air, the likeness of anything that creeps on the ground, the likeness of any fish that is in the water under the earth" (Deut 4:15–18). In other words, only God is in control of all those beasts, no matter how impressive or frightening they look. They are mere creatures themselves, certainly not deities. Don't bow or kneel to them! Genesis 1 is actually more like a confession of faith in the "real" God.

As noted earlier, the *Catechism of the Catholic Church* accepts the struc-tural, symbolic interpretation of Genesis 1. The core message remains: "*Nothing exists that does not owe its existence to God the Creator.* The world began when God's word drew it out of nothingness; all existent beings, all of nature, and all human history are rooted in this primordial event, the very genesis by which the world was constituted and time begun."[14] But creation is not a one-time event in the far past, not even a moment in time, for time hadn't begun yet; creation is rather an ongoing, continuing pro-cess. That's why the seventh day hasn't ended yet. As the "Psalm of Creation" says about all creatures, "When you take away their breath, they die and return to their dust. When you send forth your spirit, they are created" (Ps 104:29–30). Such is God's perpetual role in creation, from beginning to end; he is the Alpha and the Omega.

---

14. *CCC*, no. 338.

It is worthwhile to compare the creation account of Psalm 104 with the first creation account in Genesis. They have a similar structure, but use a rather different style. With its style of praise, prayer, and hymn, the tone of Psalm 104 is less ambiguous than the misleadingly descriptive approach used in the first chapter of Genesis, and it makes it easier to see that we don't need to read biblical creation accounts as historical or scientific reports. Yet they have in common the language of praise for what God has done for his creation. What God has done is well done!

I hope this comparison may help you consider Genesis 1 as more like a hymn of praise—actually almost a prayer—than a historical, scientific report. Again, as Saint Augustine said, ". . . our authors knew the truth about the nature of the skies, but it was not the intention of the Spirit of God, who spoke through them, to teach men anything that would not be of use to them for their salvation." [15] Pope Leo XIII said it more concisely and clearly: "[Scientific] truths . . . do not help anyone to salvation." [16] And Jesus keeps reminding us as to what the real priorities for our salvation should be: "For what will it profit them to gain the whole world and forfeit their life?" (Mk 8:36; Mt 16:26).

All of the above does not imply in any way that we can dismiss the creation events in the Bible as mere legend. The story of the creation and fall of man is a true account, even if not written entirely according to modern literary techniques, but rather in a style of writing that Westerners do not typically use. The *Catechism* states, "The account of the fall in Genesis 3 uses figurative language, but affirms a primeval event, a deed that took place *at the beginning of the history of man.* Revelation gives us the certainty of faith that the whole of human history is marked by the original fault freely committed by our first parents." [17] We were created "good," but our original goodness became corrupted when we refused to follow God's commandments.

So the first three chapters of Genesis occupy a unique place in the Bible. As the *Catechism* puts it, "The inspired authors have placed them at the beginning of Scripture to express in their solemn language the truths of creation—its origin and its end in God, its order and goodness, the

---

15. *The Literal Meaning of Genesis*, 2:9.

16. *Providentissimus Deus*, 18.

17. *CCC*, no. 390.

vocation of man, and finally the drama of sin and the hope of salvation."[18] Creation has such a richness, offering many ways of looking at it: consider Genesis 1, Genesis 2, Psalm 104, Job 38, and others. Yet we can never capture its full meaning.

However, what the Book of Scripture reveals to us doesn't take away from what science has to tell us based on the Book of Nature. Wise King Solomon explicitly mentioned this latter source of knowledge when he said, "For it is he who gave me unerring knowledge of what exists, to know the structure of the world and the activity of the elements" (Wis 7:17). Being able to explain nature does not detract from God's glory; on the contrary, once we can explain what had puzzled us so far, we have also discovered something more marvelous about the intricate structure of God's creation—"as though God were waiting behind every door opened by science," in the words of Pope Pius XII.[19] New scientific discoveries enrich our understanding of creation, or in the words of the *Catechism*: "These discoveries invite us to even greater admiration for the greatness of the Creator, prompting us to give him thanks for all his works and for the understanding and wisdom he gives to scholars and researchers."[20]

Whereas the Book of Scripture tells us the story of creation as an explanation of where this world really comes from and why this world came into existence, the rest of the story may very well be found in the Book of Nature, telling us about the stages this world actually went through starting at the beginning of time, in order to reach the point where we are now. We have the right to hear the whole story, not just the biological part that science tells us, or the religious part that comes from faith.

Knowledge based on the Book of Nature originates from God as much as knowledge from the Book of Scripture does, for "the created world receives weight, number, and measure through the hands of God."[21] The Book of Scripture may show us how to go to heaven, but we need the Book of Nature to tell us how the heavens go. Generations of popes have taught this under the motto "Faith and Reason." These two terms constantly remind us that our minds should work in the light of

---

18. *CCC*, no. 289.

19. *Address to the Pontifical Academy of Sciences*, November 22, 1951.

20. *CCC*, no. 283.

21. Pius XI, *Address to the Pontifical Academy of Sciences* in 1939.

reason as well as in the light of faith. Reason may help us better understand the God of our faith, just as faith in God may help us better
understand the structure of the universe. The *Catechism* puts it this way:
". . . the things of the world and the things of faith derive from the same
God."[22] But we should never read the Book of Scripture as if it were the
Book of Nature, or vice versa. Scientific discoveries and research have
helped us enormously to get a better and better reading of this Book of
Nature, for science has often been a candle to light the dark side of nature.
What does the Book of Nature tell us when we ask, "Where do we come
from?" We'll find out in the next chapter.

========================= DELVING DEEPER =========================

## The Book of Scripture and the Book of Nature

The Catholic Church has always distinguished between the Book of
Scripture and the Book of Nature. As Saint Augustine said: "It is the divine
page that you must listen to; it is the book of the universe that you must
observe."[23] Beginning with the apostolic writers, many Christian authors
realized that reading the divine pages of the Book of Scripture had to be
associated with observing the Book of Nature (or the universe).

Galileo also used the metaphor of the two books to defend the compat-
ibility of his heliocentric system with Sacred Scripture. Nature and
Scripture were presented by Galileo as two books proceeding from the
same divine Word; therefore, the glory of God can also be known by means
of the works that he has written in the "open book of heaven." Galileo did
mention, though, that this "book cannot be understood unless one first
learns to comprehend the language and read the letters in which it is composed"[24] (Galileo is referring to the language of mathematics).

Johannes Kepler, a contemporary of Galileo, also spoke of the Book of
Nature as a book in which God reveals himself in another way than he is

---

22. *CCC*, no. 159.

23. Augustine, *Enarrationes in Psalmos*, 45, 7.

24. Letter to Maria Cristina of Lorraine, 1615.

revealed in the Sacred Scriptures. Kepler was convinced that God created the world according to an intelligible plan accessible through the light of reason.

Pope John Paul II's encyclical *Fides et Ratio* (Faith and Reason) revived this dialogue between the two books. Pope Benedict XVI reinforced the same message when he said, "Galileo saw nature as a book whose author is God in the same way that Scripture has God as its author. It is a book whose history, whose evolution, whose 'writing' and meaning, we 'read' according to the different approaches of the sciences."[25]

---

25. Benedict XVI, Address to the Pontifical Academy of Sciences, 2008.

———◇◆◇———

# CHAPTER 3

# Where We Come From—
# According to Science

## 3.1 Is Evolution a Fact?

If we want to take reason seriously—with science being one of its products and tools—we need to know what scientists claim when they say there is such a thing as evolution. I am not talking yet about the *mechanism* of evolution—that's where Darwinism would come in—but first of all about the *fact* of evolution. This basically means that all living entities have a common descent, in spite of changes (so-called common descent with modification). That's why evolution posits that species may alter in time, give rise to new species, or die out entirely. Life scientists offer at least seven types of evidence to show why they think species altered in time, gave rise to new species, or died out entirely.

### 1. Taxonomical evidence

Taxonomy is the science of classifying living things. How would we classify human beings in the living world? A human being is, after all, a biological animal. This does not mean that a human is merely an animal—it is an unusual, very peculiar animal, endowed with rationality and morality. Nevertheless, human beings are *animals*, having characteristics all animals share. Like all other animals, we breed, feed, bleed, and excrete; we are flesh of their flesh. If we narrow the range and zoom in further, we see that we share many more features. Humans have a skeleton like some of the animals, the *vertebrates*. In addition, humans start their lives in a womb, like some of the vertebrates, the *mammals*. Then they have a relatively large brain, which they have in common with a subgroup of the mammals, the *primates*. And they lack a tail like some of the primates, the *hominids*. As we tighten the range, the resemblances become more numerous and striking.

Therefore, we should somehow acknowledge that we all belong to the same animal family, which would turn animals such as dogs, cats, and apes into some kind of "relatives." Does this also mean that we share common ancestors? Not necessarily, but if we did, this would make much more sense of the way we fit into a classification of the animal world. Human beings do share some likeness with all animals, having more likeness to animals that are vertebrates, even more to mammals, and still more to the primates, particularly the hominids. So while we may have many relatives in the animal world, some look like close relatives and others like more distant relatives. This observation is the first indication of common descent and ancestry.

## 2. Morphological evidence

Let us take mammals as an example of close morphological similarities. All mammals share more or less the same morphological structure, in spite of obvious differences in appearance. Just the fact that all mammals have seven cervical vertebrae illustrates this point—no matter whether it is in the sturdy neck of a rhino or the long neck of a giraffe. They also share the same basic pattern in their extremities, but adjusted to specific needs. While some common basic structures may have become *over*developed, others seem rather *under*developed because they had lost their functionality in certain groups of mammals. Structures that have lost their functionality are called *rudimentary*; such "left-over" parts only make sense if we assume that all mammals derive their same build from common ancestors.

Instances of rudimentary structures are common in the mammal world. Even though it is underdeveloped, whales still have a tiny pelvis dating to when they were land mammals. We ourselves share ear muscles and an appendix with other mammals, but these have lost their original function. As a matter of fact, all mammals (including humans) still have floating ribs and vertebral processes that were most likely real ribs in their long-gone ancestors. And in the evolutionary tree of horses, fossils show that certain parts of their hoofs gradually disappeared while other parts have become prominent. All this is only a small, rather arbitrary selection of morphological evidence for common descent. These odd phenomena only make sense if we assume that all mammals have common ancestors and inherited the same basic body plan. As Darwin writes: "The framework of bones being the same in the hand of a man, wing of a bat, fin of the porpoise, and leg of the horse—the same number of vertebrae forming the neck of the giraffe and of the elephant—and innumerable other such facts, at once explain themselves on the theory of descent with slow and slight successive modifications."[1]

Even animal behavior shows traces of evolution's past. Amphibians must return to the water to lay their shell-less eggs, even those that have become land animals (such as terrestrial salamanders). Reptiles, on the other hand, must lay their eggs on land, even if they spend most of their time in water (such as sea turtles). Their evolutionary past seems to have taken its toll.

## 3. Embryological evidence

During the embryological development of organisms, we often find intermediary stages that were once final stages in ancestors. In general, if a structure predates another structure in evolutionary terms, then it also appears earlier than the other in the embryo. Human embryos, for instance, develop gill pouches just like fish, but they never become real gills; and the human cerebrum develops last. If a structure disappeared during evolution, then a corresponding structure may appear first but then disappear or become modified. Whales, for example, have no legs, but during their embryonic development, leg extremities occur, then recede; they also have hair at one stage, but lose most of it later.

In other words, when you compare the embryological development of various mammals, the beginning stages usually show a greater deal of similarity than the end stages, which may differ dramatically. Thanks to those shared beginning stages, we may often be able to trace a species' ancestry.

---

1. *Origin of Species*, 1859, ch. 14.

For example, the fact that pharyngeal gill pouches appear briefly during the early embryology of mammals, including humans, is taken to indicate that the distant ancestors of land vertebrates were aquatic. Our ancestors must have come from the water (even though apes can't swim anymore). And human embryos still develop a layer of downy hair that they shed at about thirty-five weeks of gestation. We could also say that evolution has somehow left its imprint behind. In Darwin's words, "[W]e can clearly see why the embryos of mammals, birds, reptiles, and fishes should be so closely alike, and should be so unlike the adult forms."[2] All this does not mean that human embryos as they develop are retracing the whole evolutionary history of humanity, step by step. The human embryo never has gills in any sense of the word. The fanciful notion of gills is based upon the presence of six alternating ridges and grooves in the neck region of the human embryo. While similar arches do give rise to gills in certain aquatic vertebrates such as fish, their development in mammals has nothing to do with gills or even breathing. In humans and other mammals, these arches and pouches develop into part of the face and its jaws (first arch; a faulty closing of this arch would cause a cleft palate), muscles of facial expression (second arch), some endocrine glands (third and fourth arches), and the larynx (sixth arch), whereas the fifth arch vanishes. So, a human embryo does not *become* human at some point during its development, but rather *is* uniquely human at every stage of its development—which is partially due to the fact that its DNA is human from the very start.

## 4. Paleontological evidence

Paleontologists have unearthed an immense collection of fossils, most of which come from flora and fauna very different from ours. In general, the deeper the layers from which they originate, the more their fossils differ from their current counterparts. Mammals and fruit plant fossils, for instance, occur only in higher, more recent layers (which can be independently dated by radioactive dating of rocks). In general, fossil formation has a better chance of happening in water (away from oxygen in the air), as bones are buried by sediment, sand, and other materials that settle out of the water. In time, more deposits cover the layers of mud and sand, thus

---

2. Ibid.

pressing down the layers holding the remains and hardening them into rock. Later on, changes in the earth's surface may expose parts of these layers, as when stream erosion wears away layers of sediment.

As to many types of animals, so-called evolutionary trees have been constructed showing the hypothetical connections between related fossils. In addition, we can still find existing intermediate forms between fish and reptiles (such as amphibians, which grow up in water like fish, move to land like reptiles, and come back to water to lay their eggs), or between reptiles and mammals (think of so-called living fossils such as the duck-billed, beaver-tailed, otter-footed mammal called platypus, known to lay eggs developed in a "mammalian" uterus). But researchers have also unearthed fossils of transitory stages, such as fishlike reptiles, reptilelike birds, and reptilelike mammals. The particular shape of an evolutionary tree may be up for discussion, but the tree itself is more or less a scientific fact. However, since fossilization is a relatively rare phenomenon, many connections may be missing, producing so-called missing links. Inevitably some guesswork comes in here, which leads to a more detailed tree that is less scientific than we may have hoped. Fortunately, we now have newer and better tools to assess evolutionary connections in more reliable and scientific ways (see number 5 below).

Additional evidence comes from the theory of continental drift, the idea that the current location of continents is the result of a radical transformation. Originally, all continents formed one large continent (Pangaea), but parts of it drifted away to reach their current position (the so-called *continental drift* based on plate tectonics theory). Australia, for example, had already been isolated from the other continents before mammals appeared; consequently, marsupials could flourish in Australia due to lack of mammalian competition, allowing them to show the same diversity as mammals found in the rest of the world. It would be hard to explain these odd facts without the assumption of some kind of evolutionary process.

## 5. Chromosomal evidence

Chromosomes form when a cell divides, which makes them visible in a light microscope. They are packed with DNA (more on DNA under number 6), and may contain hundreds of genes. Each species has a specific number of paired chromosomes—one half coming from the female parent and the other half from the male parent. Chimpanzees, for instance, have twenty-four pairs of chromosomes, whereas humans have only twenty-three pairs (actually twenty-two + XX for females or twenty-two + XY for males). This change from twenty-four to twenty-three pairs of chromosomes can be explained if we assume that two ancestral chromosomes have fused together to form human chromosome 2. This is even more likely since gorillas and orangutans also have twenty-four pairs, just like chimpanzees. Is there any more evidence that chromosome 2 is a head-to-head fusion of two shorter chromosomes? Yes. The tips of all primate chromosomes have a special sequence of DNA code that is rare elsewhere. This sequence is found right in the middle of our fused chromosome 2. The fusion has left its DNA imprint behind, so to speak, making it hard to explain this phenomenon without postulating common ancestry and descent. Fused chromosomes are rather common; the domestic horse (thirty-two pairs), for example, has a fused chromosome pair compared with the Prezwalski horse (thirty-three pairs).

## 6. DNA evidence

DNA is packaged into chromosomes and contains the genetic information that regulates the synthesis of enzymes and other proteins. DNA acts as a template for synthesis of messenger RNA, or mRNA, which in turn determines the order of amino acids in enzymes and other proteins. However, some DNA sections, so-called *introns*, initially are transcribed into mRNA but are then removed from the end product by *splicing*. Due to alternative splicing, a single gene may provide the code for different protein sequences. Introns may also contain "old code" that has become inactive.

Since almost all organisms contain DNA, comparing the DNA structure of different species may indicate how closely they are related. DNA is like a logbook reaching almost as far back as the origin of life. Comparing DNA from different species gives us a strong indication of common descent between organisms. But there is even better evidence based on so-called pseudogenes. These genes resemble a regular DNA packet of a functional gene, but they have been affected by one or more glitches that change their script into "nonsense." They were once functional copies of genes but have since lost their protein-coding ability (and, presumably, their biological function). In a way, pseudogenes are like rudimentary organs (see number 2 on page 36). When comparing humans and chimpanzees, we do find genes that are functional in one species but not in the other (so we call them pseudogenes). A striking example is the gene for a jaw muscle protein (MYH16), which has become a pseudogene in humans, but is still functional to develop strong jaw muscles in other primates. Another example would be the DNA sequence for an enzyme that produces ascorbic acid (vitamin C) in most animals. Many primates, including humans, have a defect in this DNA code, so they must acquire vitamin C through food—yet they hold on to its repetitive sequences in the "silent" section of their DNA. Amazing, isn't it?

## 3.2 Weighing the Evidence of Evolution

Do the aforementioned reasons (1–6) provide enough evidence to substantiate the scientific claim of evolution? In other words, did evolution really happen? Or put differently, can we prove that there is such a thing as evolution? First of all, philosophers of science will tell you that in science nothing can be *proven* to be true beyond any doubt. Here's why.

As a general rule, research goes through a distinct process often called the *empirical cycle*. Research starts with some given *facts*; what scientists call a fact is actually an observation that has been repeatedly confirmed and is commonly accepted as true. Based on these facts, scientists come up with a *hypothesis* to explain these facts. From this hypothesis follow certain other *implications* that were not known yet. By testing these implications in the field or in the lab, scientists find new *facts* that either confirm or falsify the hypothesis under investigation. Hypotheses can subsequently be used to build more complex inferences and explanations, thus eventually gaining the status of a theory. Because of this empirical cycle, science is a *tentative* enterprise, leading to acceptance, revision, or rejection of a hypothesis. What is accepted as a fact today may be modified or even discarded tomorrow. Science never ends, because the empirical cycle is a never-ending, circular process. Don't confuse this with a vicious circle; the empirical cycle is more of a spiral than a circle.

So, science stands or falls by deriving test implications from its hypotheses. The outcome of each test implication can go one of two ways: The test decides either *for* or *against* the hypothesis; in other words, the hypothesis either makes true predictions or false predictions. Therefore, science has an important rule for hypotheses if they are to be of any use: They must have *observational* consequences for them to qualify as scientific. Scientific research is like a dialogue between the possible and the actual, between fiction and reality, between invention and discovery. If the test implication comes true, we receive more *confirmation*; but if the test implication cannot be confirmed, we speak of *falsification*. Apparently, confirmation leads us to probable knowledge, but never to certain knowledge; at the very most, scientific knowledge is of a highly probable nature, but it is never one hundred percent certain. Put differently, *confirmation* never reaches the status of *verification*. Alas, there is no certitude in the empirical sciences.

Did you read this right? Yes, let me repeat it: We can never prove a hypothesis to be absolutely true for the simple reason that universal, law-like statements (and that's what hypotheses usually are) hold for an unlimited, infinite number of cases—past, current, and future, seen as well as unseen. In science, we need more than "anecdotal" evidence. However, there is just no logically guaranteed way of reasoning from *some* singular instances to *all* possible cases. *Verification* is an unattainable goal; attaining certain knowledge is beyond a scientist's reach. The most scientists can claim is that the hypothesis is extremely likely after they have studied many similar cases. Such an outcome is called *confirmation*, but this leads to probable, but never certain knowledge.

But we have another problem: The same fact can be explained by different hypotheses. So we would still need falsification in order to eliminate the wrong hypothesis (and both may even turn out to be wrong). Falsification leads to the elimination of those hypotheses that have not stood up to the test of confirmation; it is a great tool to weed out false hypotheses. Science may not be able to prove, but it can disprove.

Indeed, falsification is a logically safe and better way of reasoning, in this way: If the hypothesis is true, its implication must also be true; but if the implication turns out *not* to be true, then the hypothesis *must* be false. This gives us reason to conclude that, in general, falsification is a vital and safe tool in science. No wonder, then, that science has this important methodological rule saying that hypotheses and theories should be falsifiable (i.e., testable in the sense of refutable)—which is basically a gate-keeping rule to keep unscientific statements out. Albert Einstein used to say that no amount of experimentation could ever prove him right; but a single experiment could prove him wrong.[3] That is how science learns from its mistakes.

However, the requirement of falsifiability in the empirical sciences doesn't imply that a *falsifiable* hypothesis or theory is automatically *falsified* on the first hit. There may be several reasons why counterevidence is not always accepted as falsifying evidence. One of the main reasons is that the validity of any counterevidence can always be questioned, since all evidence is based on interpretation. So ultimately, evidence depends on verification. But if final verification is beyond our reach, so is falsification. Therefore, it is always possible to reject the counterevidence as spurious. However, no matter what, we still can learn from falsification.

So we are back at the very facts that we started with, but not necessarily the same facts that we began the cycle with. We are dealing here with a game of questioning and answering, of searching and testing that is basically a trial and error or hit and miss strategy. We hit with a hypothesis and learn from each miss. We ask nature a question couched in a hypothesis, and nature gives us an answer phrased in test results. So, some of the facts that we started with may have to be replaced with revised facts that serve as a basis for the next cycle. One could actually make the case that what we call proven scientific knowledge is only proven until a new set of empirical data disprove what was previously considered proven. Francis Crick, one of the two scientists who discovered the structure of DNA, is often quoted as saying that a theory that fits all the facts is bound to be wrong, as some of the facts will be wrong.

Let's apply all we have learned so far to our main issue, evolution (we are not discussing its mechanism yet). The hypothesis is that all species have common ancestors, or common descent. Although several Greek philosophers had already adopted this idea, the hypothesis got a real boost with William Harvey's claim that all life emerges from life ("*omne vivum ex ovo* [or *vivo*]"), so there wouldn't be any life without "parents." From then on (1651), evolutionary ideas were set out by a few natural philosophers including Pierre Maupertis in 1745, Erasmus Darwin in 1796, and Jean-Baptiste Lamarck in 1800. Charles Darwin formulated his idea of

3. See Albert Einstein, *Collected Papers of Albert Einstein*, vol. 7, Document 28. The Berlin Years: Writings, 1918–1921, eds. M. Janssen, R. Schulmann, et al. (Princeton: Princeton University Press, 2002).

natural selection (as a mechanism of evolution) in 1838; he was still developing his theory in 1858 when Alfred Russell Wallace sent him a similar theory, so Darwin rushed to publish his book in 1859.

The hypothesis of evolution was the result of a mental leap based on many "facts" found in nature. It does what any hypothesis is supposed to do—it unifies a diversity of facts. In this case it assumes that all forms of life have parents and, therefore, are based on common descent with modification. In doing this, the hypothesis (or theory) of evolution makes sense of the many facts we discussed in the previous chapter, coming from paleontology, embryology, morphology, biochemistry, genetics, and so forth. As the Harvard biologist Ernst Mayr put it: "The theory of evolution is quite rightly called the greatest unifying theory in biology."[4] Isn't that exactly what a scientific hypothesis is meant to do—unify? That's why Columbia University geneticist Theodosius Dobzhansky (1900–1975) used to point out that nothing in biology makes sense except in the light of evolution. The diversity of organisms and their patterns of distribution would make for a bewildering chaos of disparate facts until unified and given sense by the theory of evolution. Science is a perpetual search for unity behind seeming diversity, for order behind seeming chaos, for regularity behind apparent irregularity.

As with any hypothesis, we should be able to find examples confirming the hypothesis. And that's what biologists have been doing ever since Darwin published his hypothesis. I will mention only a few examples. One is that the earlier embryological stages of different species are expected to be more similar than the final stages, and this has been confirmed again and again. Another is the existence of rudimentary organs and pseudogenes, which are hard to explain without the hypothesis of evolution. A third example concerns fossils: fossils of invertebrates predate fossils of vertebrates, those of reptiles predate mammals, those of marsupials predate placentals, and so forth. A fourth example is that closely related species exist in adjoining localities. A fifth example is that species in isolated locations differ from mainland species. Over and over, biologists have confirmed these observations that imply evolution.

So far we have only focused on *confirmation*. But is the theory of evolution open to *falsification* as well? Or is it basically unbeatable? The theory

---

4. Ernst Mayr, *Populations, Species, and Evolution.* (Boston: Harvard University Press, 1970), 1.

is certainly falsifiable, at least potentially. The theory of common descent would be falsified, for example, if humans had blue blood (like lobsters do, based on hemocyanin instead of hemoglobin), if they didn't have mitochondria (the cell's "batteries"), or had chromosomes packed with RNA (instead of DNA). It would be falsified if apes didn't have DNA more similar to ours than birds do, or if we would ever find a fossil rabbit in layers from the Precambrian era, or a fossil giraffe in Australia. It would also be falsified if we were to find true chimeras combining parts from different lineages (similar to centaurs and mermaids)—for instance, lobsters with bones, or fish with an outer skeleton.

The next question is whether in fact evolutionary scientists have ever encountered real *falsification*? Did the hypothesis (or call it theory if you will) ever make false predictions? Yes, it did, especially in its early stages, because disciplines such as genetics, embryology, and molecular biology were not developed enough. Many biologists at the time wanted to find falsifying evidence, but advances in science made it possible to explain these instances as merely illusive counterevidence. One of these seeming falsifications was the phenomenon of altruism in animal behavior, until biologists were able to explain this fact as well. Another one might be the problem of irreducible complexity (as claimed by *Intelligent Design* theorists), but I will argue later that this is not really a case of falsification (see page 111, 4.3). Then there is the problem of "missing links" in evolution. Should we take those as falsifying evidence? Or should we follow a different strategy and assume that some evolutionary changes happened so abruptly that their chances of being fossilized were quite small? Most biologists would opt for the latter—and rightly so.

As to be expected, some serious riddles are still left—the origin of sexuality being one of them, and perhaps the origin of life. Yet, the theory of common descent with modification appears to be well established. I would even dare to say that the theory of evolution has actually "evolved" from a theory into a fact. As Pope Benedict XVI put it, "there are many scientific tests in favor of evolution."[5]

Yet a handful of biologists keep maintaining that evolution has not occurred. Shouldn't we take them seriously? I don't think so, but I must

---

5. Benedict XVI, Meeting with the clergy, July 26, 2007. The Pope said that he is puzzled by the current debate in the United States and his native Germany over creationism and evolution.

admit I am a bit biased and may have been indoctrinated beyond repair (according to some) with the concept of evolution during my studies. All I can come up with is the following comparison (forgive me for using this analogy): Aren't there still some people, even a few historians, who deny the Holocaust? And aren't there people who still deny that humans have ever landed on the moon? And even thought there are, should we really give them our time and attention? I would say, don't bother.

Sometimes, comparisons may help us take the edge off the debate. Compare this discussion with the study of languages such as Greek, Latin, and Sanskrit. Should we believe that they were already in existence from the very beginning of humanity, or is it more reasonable to assume that they have sprung from some common source that may no longer exist? Wouldn't we all prefer the latter? My guess is that even creationists would allow for some form of evolution in this case.

Later on we will get back to this thorny issue. For now, I say only this: Claiming that evolution is merely a theory or hypothesis may be technically correct, but that holds for any kind of scientific theory. So it is not very relevant to our discussion. As a matter of fact, everything seems to indicate that evolution has indeed evolved from a hypothesis into a fact. Isn't it ironic that we have no problem saying that our children must have gotten certain genes from their grandparents, yet it is hard for some of us to acknowledge that they also received some mammalian genes from long gone mammalian ancestors? Genes connect us with the origin of life through a long line of common descent, starting from long before Adam and Eve. Somehow we have to accept that, compared with the rest of the animal world, we are "bone of their bone, flesh of their flesh, and blood of their blood"—albeit with much modification. In that sense, we all come from "the dust of the earth."

## 3.3 The Mechanism of Evolution

Let us assume from now on that we do accept evolution as an established fact. I hope I have given you enough evidence to claim that there is a common ancestry among organisms, with species giving rise to new species. Once we accept this, we have to look under the hood of evolution and come up with a mechanism that explains exactly how species can multiply and change over time. Many scientists have tried to do so, but the winning horse in the race seems to have come from Charles Darwin (1809–1882). He is the one who hypothesized the mechanism of natural selection (although there is more to it). Darwin's theory of natural selection basically attempts to explain nature's beautiful design in terms of causality—without invoking Designer interventions.

Let me explain. Unlike other natural sciences, the life sciences study phenomena not only in relation to their (physical) *causes*, but also in relation to their (biological) *functions*—that is, in relation to their effects on survival (which is also called *teleology*).

For example, because the caterpillars of a white cabbage butterfly are green rather than white (which is caused by certain genes), their camouflage makes these slow organisms feeding on green cabbage less conspicuous to predators. Thus they are more successful in surviving and reproducing. In cases like these, we are not as much interested in the *causes* of camouflage (such as genes) as we are in its *effects* on survival. Biological features can be understood in terms of their effects—that is, in terms of survival problems that need to be effectively solved. In other words, they serve a *function*; the function of the green color of a caterpillar is to deceive potential predators. That is their end or goal—or in more neutral, biological terms, their *function*. You could also say that camouflage is for deceiving, just as a knife is for cutting. Green caterpillars achieve a goal, however, without having that goal as a purpose in mind; they are just born that way. So they have *functions* but not *intentions*. Intentions and purposes may be something in the mind of a human product maker, but functions and designs are a feature of the product itself.

Where did the design come from? Was it drafted by a divine Designer? Darwin did not really go into this discussion, but rather looked for a causal, physical explanation based on past history. In his quest for causality and for natural laws, he came up with the mechanism of natural selection. Natural selection promotes good designs more than bad designs, which increases their frequency in future generations. Hence the reasoning goes basically as: The green color causes camouflage; camouflage is a successful design; therefore natural selection promotes this functional causality. In other words, the green color of caterpillars has a selective advantage over other colors, and therefore increases its frequency through better reproduction.

In short, natural selection is the causal, physical mechanism based on nature's functionality and design. Natural selection favors biological designs that solve a problem posed by the environment. The more an organism is adapted to its environment—making for a better design fit to solve a problem posed by the environment—the more likely this organism is to contribute to the genetic constitution of the next generations. Don't think this is an explanation of past causes in terms of future goals; if those future goals are successful, then natural selection promotes its past causes. That seems to be a law of nature. Somehow, natural selection promotes the better designs by weighing the benefits against the costs, much like an engineer, economist, or architect.

Natural selection works on (genetic) variation and promotes the designs that are more successful, adapted, effective, and goal-directed than others. So Darwin came up with a physical explanation based on material causes, since he considered it his scientific duty to come up with "physical" causes and "natural" laws.

The question, however, is whether Darwin fully achieved that goal. The answer is yes and no. He certainly came up with a scientific explanation, and in that sense he did succeed. He was well aware that science should search for a lawful evolutionary mechanism similar to the mechanisms many astronomers and physicists had already discovered in their respective fields. As he said in one of his letters, "astronomers do not state that God directs the course of each comet and planet."[6] What a great insight Darwin had: comets and planets follow laws of nature, and that should also be the case for evolution.

In another sense, Darwin did not succeed, for he ignored the following questions: Why do certain biological designs work, being successful and effective in reaching their goals? What makes them goal-directed? What carries them through the filter of natural selection? True, these are not biological but *meta*physical (the prefix "meta" is italicized here to emphasize that these questions are located in a realm beyond or surpassing the physical realm). That doesn't mean that those questions don't exist but that, as a scientist, Darwin had to leave such questions untouched.

*Teleology* comes in here. Teleology is about goal-directed phenomena. The biological world displays teleology because the animate world is designlike. Similarly, teleology is found in the world of technology, because that world is designlike as well. However, these two worlds have a fundamental

---

6. In correspondence with geologist Charles Lyell in 1861.

difference. In the technical world, the goal of a design is also a purpose in the designer's mind. In the biological world, on the other hand, the goal of a design is not a purpose in some animate "mind"; caterpillars, for instance, achieve a goal without having a "purpose in mind"; they were just born that way. Why were they born that way? Because natural selection promoted such a biological design. So we are back at teleology.

Most biologists feel uncomfortable with the idea of teleology. The physiologist Ernst Von Brücke used a rather risky but telling analogy when he said that biologists treat teleology like a lady they cannot live without but are ashamed to be seen with in public. And this very teleology leaves us some thorny *meta*physical questions. Even if we acknowledge that a heart works because it is designed like a pump, and that an eye works because it is designed like a camera, we still have to face some *meta*physical questions: Why does a pump or a camera work at all? In other words, natural selection may explain *that* a fine working design has a better chance of being reproduced, but ultimately it cannot explain *why* such a design is working so well. That's where teleology comes in, for *design* is a teleological concept.

The *meta*physical answer to these questions is that a heart and a pump work because they follow the laws and constraints laid down in the *cosmic* design of creation. The universe has an overall set of restraints harnessing individual designs. Without a *meta*physical design in the background, biological (as well as technological) designs could not work at all. The most perplexing thing about a watch is not so much that someone invented such a design but that the universe allows for any kind of design to work the way it works, thus making certain designs more goal-directed and more successful than others—which is a matter of teleology again.

So where do purpose and design come from? Somehow they must have been built into nature—as some kind of all-pervasive, goal-directed architecture. Successful biological designs have something that carries them through the filter of natural selection. In other words, natural selection on its own cannot do the job unless it works within a framework of cosmic design. Without this cosmic design, there could be no (natural) selection. Natural selection can only favor those specific *biological* designs that follow the rules of the *cosmic* design (by the way, designers, engineers, and architects must do the same thing).

Darwin may have thought he could reduce teleology to causality, but his causality mechanism of natural selection can only work on condition that teleology exists in nature. Darwin may have believed that he took "purpose" out of science by explaining it in terms of a "physical mechanism"— and in a way he did—but at the same time he left it in as a *meta*physical presupposition. Leon Kass, M.D., chairman of the President's Council on Bioethics from 2001 to 2005, couldn't have said it better: Organisms "are not teleological because they have survived; on the contrary, they have survived (in part) because they are teleological."[7] In other words, the causality of natural selection doesn't *explain* teleology, but *assumes* it. So Darwin explained survival and evolutionary change by using teleology, but he didn't explain teleology itself. The cosmic design determines which designs are possible, and then it "selects" those designs that fit best. The cosmic design contains the laws and constraints that determine which biological designs are successful in reproduction and survival (in a way similar to how they determine which bridges are successful designs).

Prior to any talk of evolutionary theory, William Paley (1743–1805) had argued that something as beautifully designed as the universe must have had a Designer, just as a watch does. In the footsteps of Paley, Darwin also saw successful designs in nature, but unlike Paley, he viewed nature as something designed by the test of natural selection during a process of evolutionary change (rather than by the handwork of a Designer). George Bernard Shaw once said that Charles Darwin threw Paley's watch into the ocean. Well, Shaw was wrong. Darwin did throw away Paley's watchmaker, but certainly not his legendary watch. If he did throw something away, it was Paley's design-Designer, but not the design concept. Make no mistake: The artifact analogy of *design* is as basic to Darwinism as it is to Paley's natural theology. Since the heart is designed like a pump, it is a successful design for circulating blood. Apparently, Darwin did not discard design and what comes with it, teleology. After Darwin, the heart still existed for circulation; the *cause* of its existence may have been different, but its teleology was not. Somehow, Darwin learned to live with the teleological concept of "design" because without it, he couldn't have natural selection do its work of selecting the best design for a specific goal, purpose, or end. In other words, natural selection does not *explain* design, but by *assuming*

---

7. Leon R. Kass, M.D., "Teleology, Darwinism and the Place of Man: Beyond Chance and Necessity?" in *Toward a More Natural Science* (New York: Free Press, an imprint of Simon & Schuster, 1988), chapter 10.

design, it can explain which specific biological designs made it in evolution. When removing purpose from biology, Darwin left its imprint behind.

For now, I want to stress that natural selection promotes *optimal* designs—which are usually not *perfect* designs. They can actually become *outdated* designs in Darwin's theory (designs that lost their "purpose" and became rudimentary), because natural selection works under constantly changing circumstances. For example, a feature such as the pelvis of whales lost its function when whales moved to the ocean; and on land, swimbladders may have changed into lungs. All that matters for an optimal design is reproductive success. Success breeds success!

But again, an "optimal" design is usually not a "perfect" design, because compromises must be made in balancing costs and benefits. Organisms live with built-in boundaries caused by their ancestral history and many other genetic and developmental constraints, which puts each specific design in a straitjacket, so to speak. And then there are those constraints found in the *cosmic* design. As a consequence, designs are often far from perfect, but they are the best we can get for the time being. Natural selection goes for the best available design under the given circumstances (as a result, designs good for life in the Sahara may not be good for life in Alaska, and designs good for living in trees may not be good for living on the ground, and so on). Due to genetic differences (caused by mutations), organisms differ in design, which allows natural selection to treat them selectively. Because organisms differ in *biological* designs (genetic diversity), natural selection can promote those designs that are better in terms of the *cosmic* design.

## 3.4 Evidence for the Theory of Natural Selection

Evidence for the mechanism of natural selection is plentiful. Not only do we see its powerful effects in the wide variety of cats and dogs (the result of "artificial" or human selection), but we also see their impact all over nature.

Here is a classical example: When industrial areas in England became more polluted, the composition of the peppered moth population changed. Originally, the vast majority of peppered moths had light coloration, which effectively concealed them against the light-colored trees and lichens they rested upon (camouflage). As a result of widespread pollution, many of the lichens died out, and the trees became blackened by soot, causing the light-colored moths to die off from predation. At the same time, darker-colored moths flourished because of their ability to hide on the darkened trees, so they produced relatively more offspring carrying this genetic feature. Apparently, natural selection caused a shift in moth coloration (although critics have objected that color camouflage would not protect against bats since they prey at night).

Many other examples seem to confirm the theory of natural selection. Here is a small sample:

❖ Nearly all *Staphylococcus* bacteria are currently resistant to most antibiotics; originally only a few must have been, but after years of exposure to antibiotics, the minority became the majority. The resistant bacteria produce an enzymatic protein—probably produced by previously "silent" DNA duplicates—that effectively deactivates the antibiotic (e.g. penicillinase breaks open and thus deactivates a four-atom ring in the penicillin molecule).

❖ Blood type O (lacking A- or B-antigens) arose early in human evolution, but became prevalent, probably through its selective advantage under the pressure of malaria.

❖ A dark human skin has a selective advantage in climates with strong ultraviolet radiation, protecting the skin from developing cancer. A lighter skin, on the other hand, would be more advantageous in northern regions where sunlight is rare, because a light pigmentation allows sunlight to produce more vitamin D, thus preventing rickets.

We needn't spend any more time on these well-known cases of natural selection, because they are all located within the boundaries of the species. But that's not where the real problem lies for evolutionary theory. If it's true that a species is characterized by reproductive isolation, we should ask ourselves how a new species could ever have another species as its parent? In other words, how can a species change into a new species?

So the real problem arises when the theory of natural selection tries to deal with evolution *beyond* the boundaries of species: How does a new species evolve? Can natural selection achieve this? This phenomenon is called *speciation*. No matter how long we keep applying natural selection to our enormous variety of dogs, all individuals remain part of the same species and can still interbreed with other members of their species. Critics of the theory of natural selection keep hammering on this point; they stress that the fruit fly *Drosophila melanogaster*, for instance, may undergo very noticeable, dramatic mutations, but those mutant flies remain members of the same species because they can still mate with other members of their species. Wouldn't this seeming stability of a species demonstrate that all species are permanent and set forever, they ask? Doesn't this indicate a clear case of falsification?

I often hear laypeople say that no one has ever seen new species emerge in the laboratory, or even in nature. Does that falsify the theory? I don't think so, for several reasons. The first is that hybrids tell us that speciation may be a process that has begun but is not yet finalized. A second reason is that cases of actual speciation have been found in the lab. Another reason is that we know of new species with fused chromosomes (like our chromosome 2) or genes transferred to different chromosome sections, or that have newly inserted repetitive DNA segments. Such changes may at some point prevent pairing and mating, and thus would isolate their carriers reproductively.

But a more general reason invalidates the objections of those skeptics. Claiming that we have never observed, in nature or in the laboratory, a canyon being carved out by a river is not a fair allegation because we are dealing with a gradual, time-consuming process, far beyond our lifespan. Biologists should use a similar line of reasoning for a process such as speciation: It is often a long, winding, large-scale, step-by-step process—too slow for us to see the effect of changes, too gradual to locate any clear thresholds, and too massive to be simulated in the lab. As Pope Benedict pithily put it, "We cannot haul 10,000 generations into the laboratory."[8]

However, we have plenty of *indirect* indications that speciation has occurred in nature. The diversity of species in the Galapagos Islands (Darwin's "lab") has become a classical example, especially the huge variety of finches spread out over the many islands. Charles Darwin argued that populations on separate islands may have been isolated long enough to develop major differences that transformed them into a new species before related populations moved in; but from then on, they could no longer

---

8. Stephan Otto Horn, ed. *Creation and Evolution: A Conference with Pope Benedict XVI in Castel Gandolfo* (San Francisco, Ignatius Press, 2008).

interbreed with the original population (alas, we were not there when it happened). Once a population has become reproductively isolated, speciation has become a fact.

Despite all the above, I must admit that some differences between species are so major and drastic that they cross borders not only between species but even between classes and orders in biological taxonomy. Amphibians, for example: They grow up in water (like fish), move to land (like reptiles), and come back to water to lay their eggs (like fish again). Then we have the reptiles: most of them lay eggs, but some species simply retain the eggs until just before hatching while others provide all nutrients via a structure similar to the mammalian placenta. Or consider the still existing intermediate form of the platypus, a duck-billed, beaver-tailed, otter-footed mammal that lays eggs developed in a mammalian uterus.

Indeed, in terms of the synthetic theory, it is very difficult to explain the transition from fish to reptiles (which is definitely more than changing swim bladders into lungs, or fins into legs), from reptiles to birds (which is, again, more than changing legs into wings), and so on. The *gradualism* of Darwinism seems to fail us here (although it does allow for variations in evolutionary speed). But the still-controversial idea of *saltationism* might help us to think in terms of not only small changes but also large leaps. Saltationism refers to wide-ranging mutations that would lead to new species fairly quickly. Currently, it is hard to demonstrate such large-scale mutations. In Darwin's time, the field of genetics did not yet exist to back up his claim of gradual modification. Today genetics does support Darwin's claim, but not in a way that would open the black box of sweeping genetic changes. Yet, the idea of saltationism may not be too far-fetched because genetic programs not only contain "blueprint" genes but also instructions for processing the blueprint. The Y-chromosome of males, for instance, carries hardly any blueprint genes for specific characteristics, yet this chromosome has quite an impact on the process of sexual differentiation, as we know from rare cases when it's missing (people with Turner's syndrome have only X, which is rendered as XO, with O standing for a missing chromosome).

Saltationism may still be a controversial topic, but think of it along the following lines: Adaptations may be variations of a common structure—say, the external skeleton of insects versus the internal skeleton of vertebrates—but it is doubtful whether the structure itself also is an adaptation. Having certain characteristics such as a certain eye color or skin color may depend on genes, but having certain feature such a having an eye or a spine may not. The best explanation of this difference is probably found in the fact that a genotype is more than a genome. A genome is just a cluster of genes, but a genotype is the blueprint of a genome plus the instructions for processing the blueprint. In other words, a gene does what the program dictates—not the other way around. The program doesn't do what a gene dictates. Unfortunately, the "genetics of the genotype" is currently not as well developed as the genetics of the genome.

With his notorious "blind spot" for discontinuity, Darwin kept stressing that nature doesn't make big leaps, yet nature is actually full of giant leaps. Sometimes small genetic changes may have far-reaching effects. The extensive metamorphosis from caterpillar to butterfly, for instance, is often controlled by a single gene. Another sweeping effect of a simple mutation can be found in humans with the gene called FOXP2, discovered in a single family in England where members had severe difficulty in speaking. As it turned out, these affected members had a single letter of the DNA code "misspelled" in the FOXP2 gene on chromosome 7. But the story doesn't end here. This gene has been remarkably stable in almost all mammals—except for humans, where two significant changes occurred some hundred thousand years ago. Not only do the human and chimp versions of FOXP2 look different, but they function differently as well. The FOXP2 gene switches other genes on and off, thus driving target genes to behave differently in both species. It could very well be that all these seemingly minor genetic changes had a major impact on the development of language.

I will conclude this discussion of the evidence for evolution by quoting Pope John Paul II regarding evolutionary theory: "The convergence in the results of these independent studies—which was neither planned nor sought—is in itself a significant argument in favor of this theory."[9]

I hope you have found the evidence for evolution and its mechanism convincing.

---

9. *Address to the Pontifical Academy of Sciences*, October 22, 1996.

# 3.5 What Science Cannot Claim

Science has claimed a lot, but there are many things it cannot possibly assert. Hence, it is important for us to realize the limitations of science. Students in our schools deserve to be taught genuine science, which entails that we must also make its limitations clear. We should teach science, not preach it.

Why do so many scientists seem unaware of the limitations of their scientific claims? I confess that I have come a long way myself, because during my training as a scientist, I was hardly ever taught to look beyond the boundaries of science. Nowadays, studying a specific science takes so much time that almost none is left for other issues; besides, those teaching science usually want to stress its power, not its weaknesses. I had to discover the limitations of science myself, with God's help. An added problem is that science cannot be studied by scientists from within. In order for us to study science—its internal structure, its foundations, as well as its limitations—we need to adopt a bird's-eye view, a so-called metalevel, a philosophical perspective, a metaphysical viewpoint—a science of science, if you will. Unfortunately, it seems many scientists have never reached such a "high altitude." They tend to stare at that square inch, nanometer, or micron they are working on and feel comfortable with it, while forgetting that so much more surrounds it. They work so hard that they have hardly any time left for serious thinking.

So let's take a bird's-eye view and investigate a series of claims that science cannot make, even though such claims have been very popular among both scientists and laypeople who lack a sound understanding of the nature of scientific research and its built-in limitations. The next section will discuss at least eight of those invalid and illegitimate claims. Hopefully it will help you gain a better understanding of the strengths as well as the weaknesses of scientific research. This analysis will produce some important no-trespassing signs in science that every reasonable person should respect, yet are violated daily by many.

## 1. Scientific theories are not definitive

Science cannot claim . . . that its theories are final and definitive; its "facts" may change at any time in the future. So far, no alternative theories for an evolutionary mechanism have turned up, or at least the scientific community has not adopted them as serious candidates. Nonetheless, we can predict that science will never reach final answers, no matter what individual scientists tend to think. The reason for this limitation is simple, yet conclusive: In the empirical sciences, nothing can be proven to be absolutely true beyond any doubt; and the same facts could very well be explained by different hypotheses or theories (which can't be all true). So we may find a lot of confirmation, but never complete verification; and even falsification is often not definitive, as we found out (3.2). Consequently, science is fundamentally a tentative endeavor, engaged in a never-ending spiral of searching for the truth. This empirical cycle shows us that what we call proven scientific knowledge is only proven until a new set of empirical data disprove what was previously considered proven. Whatever is accepted as a fact today may be modified or even discarded tomorrow—for science never ends its empirical cycle. At the same time, falsification allows science to learn continually from its mistakes.

Nevertheless, some scientists cannot resist the temptation to claim certainty and finality, as we all know. The Dutch physicist Pieter Zeeman, later to become a Nobel laureate, was fond of telling how in 1883, when he had to choose what to study, people had strongly dissuaded him from studying physics. "That subject's finished," he was told, "there's no more to discover." It is even more ironic that this also happened to Max Planck, since it was he who, in 1900, laid the foundations for one of the greatest leaps in physics, the quantum revolution. And as if scientists never learn, Stephen Hawkins ended his inaugural lecture some years ago by stating that it is quite possible that physics is almost finished. Apparently, it remains a timeless temptation to claim that the unknown has been reduced to almost nothing. However, the magnitude of the unknown is, well . . . unknown! The unknown is still in darkness, until we have the right searchlights to help us see. The physicist John A. Wheeler, who coined the term *black hole*, said, "We live on an island surrounded by a sea of ignorance. As our island of knowledge grows, so does the shore of our ignorance."[10]

Perhaps many biologists would like to consider the theory of natural selection a closed chapter as well—but nothing is final in science. Some

---

10. Quoted in Clifford A. Pickover, *Wonders of Numbers* (New York: Oxford University Press, 2000), 195.

people actually think a superior alternative has already been found in the theory of creationism or the theory of Intelligent Design. I will explain later why I don't think those claims are legitimate, either. This is not to say that there will never be other and better alternatives looming on the horizon. But for now, I would like to go with the reigning hypothesis of natural selection, because I cannot go with some theory that we don't know yet (but I almost dare to bet there'll be one). Pope John Paul II was right in saying, "this hypothesis proposes only a probability, not a scientific certainty"[11]; yet, he also states, "new findings lead us toward the recognition of evolution as more than a hypothesis." [12]

## 2. Science cannot answer all questions

Science cannot claim that science has all the answers to all our questions. Science is neither a know-all nor a cure-all. There is no place for megalomania in science: Science may be everywhere but it is certainly not all there is. Most sciences have succeeded by creating a test-tube-like shelter in a laboratory, removed from the complexity of nature, so that the factors under investigation can be isolated and manipulated individually. The astounding successes of science have not been gained by answering every kind of question, but precisely by refusing to do so. Science has purchased success at the cost of limiting its ambition. We are used to this kind of approach, but ancient Greek scholars detested experimental intervention— they seriously doubted that observation in an unnatural, isolated, forced experiment could be true to nature. Their reasoning went like this: By bending nature to one's own will, how could one ever discover its true features? Isolation was seen as bad practice then. How times have changed!

Nowadays, good scientists are those able to demarcate their area of investigation, able to limit themselves to factors that are relevant to what they are studying, and able to keep strict control by eliminating factors that might interfere with their search. Much of the genius of research workers lies in their selection of what is worth investigating, thus reducing their many questions to a manageable problem. Nobel laureate Peter Medawar used to describe research as a real *art*—"the art of the soluble," as he called

---

11. General audiences, January 29 and April 16, 1986.
12. *Address to the Pontifical Academy of Sciences*, Oct. 22, 1996.

it. Whatever is not yet soluble is not yet a good object of investigation. On a visit to an immunology laboratory, for instance, we would find immune cells in test tubes (*in vitro*) attacking tumor cells and producing antibodies all by themselves. This has been a successful scientific approach, since it's soluble. But this same visit may also be misleading, giving us the false impression that this is an isolated, self-regulating system, until we learn from other research that the immune system interacts extensively with other bodily systems (*in vivo*)—which fact, in turn, makes things much more complicated. Nonetheless, the test-tube approach undoubtedly makes things more "soluble."

## 3. Science is not about the entire world

Science cannot claim . . . that science is about the entire world. In a sense, each scientific field has its own outlook on the world, thus creating its own phenomena and its own facts. A psychologist has an eye for psychological phenomena, whereas a biologist perceives biological facts. Consequently, each scientific field creates its own map of the world, building a simplified and reduced version of the real world.

Maps are useful if we use the right one: a railroad map would be useless for car drivers. Consequently, we end up with a variety of maps, each one depicting a distinct aspect of the world: a geographical map, a biological map, a chemical map, an economic map, and what have you. These maps complement one another in describing and explaining disparate phenomena, which represent distinct aspects of the same world. But there is no universal map; such an all-inclusive map would be the real world itself.

Because maps and other kinds of models are abstract representations of the original world, they neglect what is out of their scope. So it is impossible to read from a map anything that was neglected as being irrelevant. That's why a map can never replace what it represents; besides, you just can't move around on a map as you can in the real world. It may sound silly to point out, but neither cobblestones nor human beings can be found on astronomical maps—they are not denied but merely neglected! Similarly, you will not find God on scientific maps, for God is outside their scope. And don't forget that maps don't give us destinations; they tell us *how* to go but not *where* to go. Destinations reside only in the minds of the mapmakers and map users.

Besides, our scientific maps are getting more and more detailed, because science is so specialized. However, "more detailed" doesn't mean "more comprehensive." We may make more and more maps that convey more and more knowledge, but unfortunately they are less and less connected. Our *uni*versities have become *multi*versities, a vast cluster of islands, each with its own specialty. Isn't it amazing how scientists like to zoom in to finer and finer details, up to a square nanometer or micron, but then tend to lose sight of the wider context? More specialization usually leads to a smaller vision of the general overview. And who is still capable of seeing the larger picture? Only God.

## 4. Science has not found a "theory of everything"

Science cannot claim . . . that science has found a "theory of everything." This limitation follows from the way that each scientific field develops its own kind of map, by focusing on what is relevant and omitting what is not.

So why do some scientists still search for the Grand Theory of Everything or, even worse, think they have found it? The atomic theory once had this disreputable aura—not only claiming that atoms are everywhere, but also that they are all there is (materialism). Later on, it became an important philosophical doctrine to declare that all living objects (including human beings) are only and merely machinelike automata (mechanicism). Then the philosopher Herbert Spencer said that everything in life is based on natural selection, including our social relationships, motives, desires, beliefs, and morals. Spencer thus exported the theory of evolution from the biological realm to the realm of sociology, psychology, and ethics. Apparently, "survival of the fittest" had become the grand new "theory of everything" for Spencer and his supporters. This amounts to saying that human beings are ultimately and exclusively driven by one thing alone—which may be natural selection, but also libido (sex), money, or whatever—thus wiping out anything else that matters in life.

In all these cases, the boundaries of the underlying theory are being grossly overstepped—thus elevating a dedicated theory to the level of a worldview, an ideology, or even a dogmatic doctrine, claiming *universal* validity for *local* successes. Whenever this happens, I would like to use the ending "-ism," so we would speak of ideologies such as atom-ism, evolution-ism, psycholog-ism, or scient-ism. All these -isms look at the world from one specific perspective, arguing that this allows us to see everything—that is, literally, *all* there is. They all suffer from some form of megalomania and essentially demand divine authority. But what gives their proponents the certainty that only their particular ideology is certain? Pope Benedict XVI was right in saying, "the doctrine of evolution does not answer all questions, and it does not answer above all the great philosophical question: From where does everything come?"[13] The astonishing successes of science have not been gained by answering every kind of question, but precisely by refusing to do so. Its success is purchased at the cost of limiting its ambition. As a consequence, anyone searching for a Grand Theory of Everything is chasing a phantom.

We could even usher in some strong mathematical help. The logician and mathematician Kurt Gödel proved in his famous so-called *incompleteness theorem* that no complex mathematical theory can be both consistent and complete; if it's consistent, it cannot be complete, for its consistency cannot be proven within the system. The late physicist Fr. Stanley Jaki, OSB, pointed out in 1966 that any "grand unified theory" will certainly be a consistent mathematical theory, and therefore must be incomplete—which would doom all searches for a deterministic Grand Theory of Everything.[14] The proof of either its consistency or its completeness must then lie outside the theory itself, which is necessarily *meta*physical territory where scientists lack competency and feel alien.

## 5. Science has not reduced the whole to its parts

Science cannot claim . . . that science has effectively reduced the whole to its parts. Here are some examples. Chemistry reduces molecules to a group of atoms; genetics reduces an organism to a collection of genes; molecular genetics reduces an organism to its DNA molecules; evolutionary biology reduces a population to a so-called gene pool. But these are only *models*—simplified replicas of the original, made for research purposes. Science typically uses a "reductionistic" approach. *Reductionism* boils down to explaining things by analyzing them into smaller and smaller

---

13. Benedict XVI, Meeting with the clergy, July 26, 2007.
14. Stanley Jaki, *The Relevance of Physics* (Chicago: University of Chicago Press, 1966), 127–130.

parts, which has been a very successful strategy in the history of science. In essence, it isolates things and uses techniques of reducing the complexity of the original to a manageable model related to a soluble problem. But this is where the danger comes in: One should not mistake a model for what it represents. No parent would consider giving a child a teddy bear if it were an exact representation of the original. The only model that could ever qualify as an exact replica of the original would be the original itself; but such an all-inclusive model is no longer a model. So, reductionism buys clarity and certitude at the price of curtailing reality.

That's why working with models can be dangerous, even if productive. Richard Dawkins, for instance, uses the gene-pool model to simulate a process of natural selection among the different variants of a gene (alleles) in a population. What we might see happening in the *model* is a change of allele frequencies. Next we might conclude that the actual unit of selection is the gene—even up to something like a "selfish gene." This approach may be fruitful—until we try to exchange the model for reality. In reality, genes are *not* units of selection. Harvard biologist Stephen Jay Gould (1941–2002) pithily rebuked, "Selection simply cannot see genes."[15] Alleles, for example, that do not come to expression in the organism cannot be subject to natural selection. In reality, the *organism* is the unit of selection, but the model may give us the misleading impression that the unit of selection is actually the *gene*. The gene is only a criterion, not a unit, of selection; it may be at center stage in the model, but certainly not in reality.

What happens when we fail to separate the model and the reality? We end up saying that an organism is really nothing but a collection of genes, that a human being is really nothing but a string of DNA, that human values are really nothing but the outcome of natural selection, that altruism is really nothing but hidden self-interest, that thinking is really nothing but a series of firings along neurons, that the unborn baby is really nothing but a blob of cells, and that a human being is really nothing but a mathematical or statistical number. Sounds familiar? Some scientists have even tried a different strategy, but with the same outcome. They state, for example, that physics always has the last word in observation, for the observers themselves are physical. But why not say that psychology always has the last word, because these observers are interesting psychological objects as

---

15. Stephen J. Gould, "Caring Groups and Selfish Genes," *Natural History*, 1977, 86(12), 20–24.

well. Either statement is nonsense; observers are neither physical nor psychological, but they can indeed be studied from a physical, biological, psychological, or statistical viewpoint, which is a different matter.

C. S. Lewis called this kind of fallacy "nothing-buttery."[16] You will often hear this myth when scientists leave their own area of expertise and blow their credentials up to immense proportions, thus becoming philosophers without any schooling in that field. Just like some movie stars, some scientists misuse their fame to promote their worldviews—or lack thereof—convinced that their scientific expertise guarantees their other beliefs.

*Neglecting* what is outside one's scope may be a wise scientific strategy, but *denying* it goes one step too far, turning into an unwarranted ideology. It's like stating that highways don't exist because they don't appear on our railroad maps. Science can never transcend or surpass itself by saying that science is all there is in the universe, for that claim would be made from outside the territory of science. It would be an illegitimate claim besides. Isn't there more to life than science? If human beings were indeed "nothing but" DNA, they would be very fragile creatures; and even this very claim would be worth nothing more than the DNA that supposedly produced it. If all we are is DNA, and we are the ones who discovered DNA, then DNA must have discovered itself!

## 6. Science and reductionism

Science cannot claim ... that its ultimate goal is a molecular explanation of life. Yet, many life scientists think they have failed as scientists if they cannot explain life in terms of its molecules. As we said before, reductionism tries to explain things by analyzing them into smaller and smaller parts. Scientists excel in this piecemeal approach. The reductionists' creed says: After dissecting them, things are much simpler than they appear. However, the first problem with reductionists is that they confuse "smaller" with "lower" (at an ontological level) and/or "simpler" (in the sense of easier to understand). But I doubt whether an atom is at a lower level or has a simpler nature than a molecule; smaller parts are not always really simpler, as quantum theory has shown us. Second, reductionists claim (without any

---

16 C. S. Lewis, *The Weight of Glory and Other Addresses*, rev. ed. (New York: Macmillan, 1980), 71–72.

justification) that explanations should always go one way, in the direction of smaller, lower, and simpler things. But if the smaller can explain the larger, why couldn't the larger explain the smaller? Would it really be better to explain the working of DNA in terms of its (smaller) *molecular* structure than in terms of its (larger) surrounding *cellular* structure? Let's find out.

The ultimate goal of most scientists seems to be to explain life in terms of DNA. Therefore, the "secret of life" is supposed to reside in DNA. In their view, DNA is the only thing that counts. So with the human genome project finished, we are supposed to know *everything* about human beings. Intuitively, we all know (or should know) better. By claiming the primacy of DNA, these scientists actually demote organisms to merely being DNA's way of creating more DNA. However, they forget that DNA is useless in itself. It is useful only if it is part of a larger, very intricate system that includes enzymes and other components located in separate cellular compartments.

I call this belief the "DNA mantra." As a matter of fact, this "miraculous" DNA is rather powerless. It can't replicate itself, and it can't even create a protein on its own. It needs all the help it can get from "outside." If DNA is put in the presence of all the pieces that will be assembled into new DNA, but without the protein machinery, nothing happens. The process is analogous to making copies of a document by an office copying machine, a process that would never be described as self-replication. DNA does not make anything, not even proteins! New proteins are made by a protein synthesis machinery that is itself made up of proteins. The role of the DNA is to specify how amino acids are to be strung together by some synthetic machinery. But this string of amino acids is not even a protein with physiological and structural functions until it is folded into a three-dimensional configuration that is partly based on its amino acid sequence, but also determined by the cellular environment and by special processing proteins. Insulin for diabetics is a case in point. Recently, the DNA coding sequence for human insulin was inserted into bacteria, so they produced a protein with the amino acid sequence of human insulin. But an amino acid sequence does not determine the shape of a protein. The first proteins harvested through this process did have the correct sequence, but were physiologically inactive. The bacterial cell had folded the protein incorrectly!

In other words, DNA is only a small link in a complex process of protein synthesis. Think of viruses, which are essentially pure DNA or RNA;

their DNA or RNA cannot do anything until they penetrate, like a Trojan horse, the interior of a living cell. The system of a cell, in turn, is part of and regulated by an even larger system—the elaborate system of an organism that switches genes on and off with hormones. As it turns out, the statement that the secret of life resides in DNA has its mirror image in the following, equally valid, yet less popular statement: life is as much the secret of DNA as DNA is the secret of life. The higher level of life, so to speak, is somehow creating what Michael Polanyi calls special "boundary conditions" for the lower-level components.[17] That's why lower-level DNA can properly function. It is harnessed inside higher-level cells, and those cells can even function better when they are harnessed within organisms at a still higher level. And that's why we can say that the secret of DNA is life—as much as the secret of life is DNA, or perhaps even more so.

## 7. Science does not operate in a vacuum

Science cannot claim . . . that science operates in a vacuum. Many scientists may think it does, but science definitely operates within a philosophical, *meta*physical framework of presuppositions. The problem is that science itself cannot be founded on scientific findings, as these presume science; its foundations must come from somewhere else. Without those pillars, science would collapse. It's the same with chess: it cannot explain its own rules.

To begin with, scientists must assume, at any moment in their research, that our universe is intelligible. But where does this notion of intelligibility come from? It certainly does not come from science itself. Scientists assume that, in principle, the world can be *known* and made intelligible—otherwise there would be no need to pursue science. Besides, for most of the sciences, this knowledge has to be expressed in a mathematical framework in order to be considered intelligible. In other words, intelligibility is definitely not the outcome of intense and extensive scientific research; it is not intra- but extra-scientific; it's a *proto*-scientific notion that must come first before science can even get started. Intelligibility can never be founded scientifically, for it actually enables science. If you were told that scientists had discovered that certain physical phenomena are *not* intelligible, you

---

17. Michael Polanyi, "Life's Irreducible Structure," *Science* 160 (3834): 1308–1312.

would, or at least should, tell them to keep trying and come up with a better hypothesis or theory—based on this fundamental philosophical assumption that says the universe is basically intelligible and comprehensible. Albert Einstein put it this way, "The most incomprehensible thing about the universe is that it is comprehensible."[18] Indeed, as far as science is concerned, the comprehensibility of the universe is definitely an incomprehensible thing, a mystery. To sum up, science must assume intelligibility, but cannot explain it.

Something similar can be said about the notions of order and causality in all of the natural sciences. It is due to these notions that science can explain and predict, which would not be possible in a world of disorder and irregularity. Again, these notions are not scientific *out*put, but rather metaphysical input; they do not come from science but they *enable* science; they are the reason for trusting our reasoning. Since we may assume that like causes produce like effects, we can explain and predict. Do not think that science has demonstrated this experimentally, for if we found that like causes produced *un*like effects, we would automatically assume that those causes must somehow be different or that some hidden causes must have interfered.

The same holds for the notion of order. Order is a *meta*physical presupposition, neither to be proved nor disproved. We can never *prove* the existence of order beyond any doubt, because order even holds for all cases to come as well as cases that could have happened but did not happen. Nor can we ever *disprove* order, because finding any exception to the rule of order does not disprove order as such, but it may falsify a specific order we had conjectured or hypothesized. In other words, the scientific rule of falsification wouldn't even work if there were no order; for it to work, it must assume order and regularity—otherwise, counterevidence would just be a case of irregularity. Apparently, order and causality do not come *from* research, but they come *before* any research can begin; they are a *given*.

Because "law and order" are given (a religious believer would say "rooted" in God's creation, for he is a trustworthy Creator), we can claim that everything has a cause and that like causes always produce like effects. But claiming that a particular phenomenon does not have a cause amounts to scientific nonsense, or actually metaphysical nonsense. Apparently, order and causality are pre- or proto-scientific, in the sense that they must come

---

18. Albert Einstein, "Physics and Reality" in *Out of My Later Years* (the Estate of Albert Einstein, 1956), 61.

first before science can follow. Consequently, "law and order" are not an *a priori* (rooted in the way we *think* about the world, à la Kant), but a *given*, rooted in the way the world *is* (which is based on creation by a lawful God). Einstein wrote, "But surely, a priori, one should expect the world to be chaotic, not to be grasped by thought in any way."[19] Einstein was enough of a philosopher to realize the importance of a *given* order, one of the main pillars of science.

Then there are the notions of design and functionality, especially in the life sciences and the technical sciences. Camouflage is for deceiving predators; a heart is for circulating blood; eye lenses are for vision. However, these features can only achieve the goal of what they are for if they have a design that leads to this goal—that is, if they are successful and effective. This means that successful biological designs have something that carries them through the filter of natural selection. What is this something that makes them work successfully and effectively? The answer to this metaphysical question is that they must have followed the rules of the cosmic design. The universe has an overall set of restraints restricting the range of possible results. As said before, a heart and a pump, or an eye and a camera, can and do work because of the way our universe has been designed and outfitted with teleology. Without a *meta*physical cosmic design in the background, they could not work at all. As a consequence, natural selection can only select those *biological* designs that are in accordance with the *cosmic* design. That is why functionality is a basic concept in the life sciences, making biologists look for the function of any biological feature—and if they can't find one, they will and should keep searching until they do. Functionality is as basic to the life sciences as causality is to all the natural sciences.

## 8. *Science cannot replace religion*

Science cannot even claim that science has replaced religion. Many scientists think it has. They claim that concepts such as the Big Bang and evolution have replaced the idea that God created the world, or they argue that medications have superceded religious prayers. Science is supposed to be an alternative to and a replacement for religion—and a much better one, in their view. If science is right, then religion must be wrong; therefore, religion is over, or at least it's on its way out—so goes the reasoning.

19. Letter to Solovine, March 30, 1952.

Whenever science makes a small step forward, religion is believed to take a small step back. You know where this is going to end . . . unless it's not true that science and religion compete with each other. Why couldn't they *complement* each other instead? Didn't we find out that creation had to come first before the Big Bang and evolution could even have gotten started? Whereas science tends to zoom in, looking for finer and finer details, religion tends to zoom out into a larger, transcending framework. Science has a piecemeal approach, dissecting things into smaller and smaller pieces, whereas philosophy and religion try to put all the pieces back together again, so we don't lose sight of the whole.

Science may be everywhere, but it certainly is not all there is, so it can't be a know-all and cure-all. Scientists are specialists, just as electricians and plumbers are specialists—they have their own expertise, nothing more and nothing less. Scientists are specialized in applying the scientific method and in using sophisticated instruments and advanced lab techniques. But this doesn't mean that scientists have some unusual, esoteric insights regarding all that's going on in the universe. Even astronomers don't deal with the entire universe, but only with its physical aspects. So let's take science off its pedestal and put it where it belongs.

And that's when religion, creation, and Adam and Eve come in, filling the void science permanently and necessarily leaves behind. Religion belongs to a territory inaccessible to science. Science and religion do not put forward rival answers to the same question, but they offer their own answers to two different kinds of questions. In other words, there's no sense giving a religious answer to a scientific question, nor a scientific answer to a religious question. Science and religion each have their own territory. As the saying goes, good fences make good neighbors; and besides, those fences keep insiders in and outsiders out. So let's respect those fences.

We should never make science a pseudoreligion, nor make religion a semi-science. As the biologist Stephen Jay Gould put it: "the *magisterium* of science covers the empirical realm: what the Universe is made of (fact) and why it works in this way (theory). The *magisterium* of religion extends over questions of ultimate meaning and moral value. These two *magisteria* do not overlap" (emphasis added).[20] They should not overlap because they are actually very different realms: Science handles the material aspects of

---

20. Stephen J. Gould, *Rocks of Ages* (New York: Ballantine Books, 2002), 207–208.

the world, whereas religion deals with its immaterial and spiritual aspects. Demanding that these two should be merged would detract from the glory of each. They are neighbors that can't live without each other.

It is very much like the concept of separation of church and state; the state should not impose a church, nor should the church impose a state. Christianity, unlike Islam, distinguishes between political and religious authorities ("Render therefore unto Caesar . . ."). The state should be protected from the church as much as the church should be protected from the state. Although state and church shouldn't interfere with each other, they should still acknowledge each other's role and authority. We need them both, but not intermingled; therefore, treat them as "church *and* state," not "church *versus* state," because they are not in *opposition* but in *composition*. In other words, render unto Caesar what is Caesar's, but never render unto Caesar what is God's.

Something similar holds true for the relationship between religion and science. They are autonomous and independent, but we need to keep them in harmony, so we don't become "schizophrenic," celebrating religion on Sundays and science on weekdays. The person of faith and the person of science are ultimately one and the same person. Together, science and religion make us whole and wholesome, whereas in isolation, they are incomplete and under-performing—with each being only one side of the coin called "faith and reason." Science should protect religion from making scientific errors, and religion should keep science within moral bounds, but never render to science what is God's. So honor the fences, but no matter on which side of the fence you happen to be, don't forget that you do have a neighbor.

---

### Summary of What Science Cannot Claim:
### Eight no-trespassing signs ("Thou shall not . . .")

| | |
|---|---|
| Science cannot claim . . . | that its theories are final and definitive |
| Science cannot claim . . . | that science has all the answers to all our questions |
| Science cannot claim . . . | that science is about the entire world |
| Science cannot claim . . . | that science has found a "theory of everything" |
| Science cannot claim . . . | that science has effectively reduced the whole to its parts |
| Science cannot claim . . . | that its ultimate goal is a molecular explanation of life |
| Science cannot claim . . . | that science autonomously operates in a vacuum |
| Science cannot claim . . . | that science has replaced religion |

## 3.6 Science and Religion: A Match Made in Heaven

For the rest of this book, I will distinguish physical causes and biological functions from mental reasons and moral values, and these in turn from transcendental notions such as grounds or origins in a philosophical context, and purposes or destinations in a religious context. This terminology may seem involved, but it helps us avoid confusion as well as questionable conclusions. Saint Albert the Great said it well when he wrote that "natural science does not consist in ratifying what others have said, but in seeking the *causes* of phenomena" (emphasis added).[21] Indeed, science attempts to explain everything in terms of physical causes and biological functions, whereas we talk about God in terms of origins and destinations (where do we come from and where do we go?). For that reason, God does not and cannot occur on scientific maps, nor can science be ruled by Scripture. In other words, do not read the Book of Nature as if it were the Book of Scripture—or vice-versa.

So let's find out how science and religion relate to each other. When the Royal Society of London for the Improvement of Natural Knowledge started its scientific activities in 1660, it officially ratified what previous scientists had started: It took the pagan concept of deity out of nature, because it considered nature to be a *created* entity—created not divine, given to us by the Creator to be studied. Thus it de-deified nature, took its quasi-divine tendencies and semihuman purposes away, and made nature a nondivine entity. When Copernicus entered the scene, "purpose" was taken out of astronomy; from Newton on, "purpose" vanished from physics; and ever since Darwin, "purpose" has been taken out of biology. Science didn't *end* up removing "purpose" from its vocabulary, but it did *start* out with "purpose" removed from its radar screen—not as a conclusion *after* extensive experimentation, but as a premise *before* any experimentation.

When scientists removed purpose from scientific discourse, they didn't make it disappear, of course; they just moved it from inside to outside the scientific domain. The fact that purposes don't exist in science doesn't mean they don't exist at all; they are not entirely out of the picture, but they are out of the scientific picture. Yet you can never simply reject what you neglect. As we all know, the direction of something like a billiard ball on

---

21. *De Mineralium et Rebus Metallicis.*, lib. II, tr. ii, i.

the pool table is ruled not only by physical laws but also by human intentions and other purposes in life. However, once purpose has been eliminated from science, it can no longer be explained by science, so it is forever beyond the reach of science.

Hence, it shouldn't surprise us that some laypeople think this de-deification has taken the splendor out of nature. The rainbow, for instance, used to be "God's prerogative," until science could explain such an effect in terms of refraction of light—which then allowed us to play the "trick" ourselves (with a garden hose and a spotlight). Why do people feel robbed? The answer is that they had God do what science can explain now, so in their eyes, science took away from God what was believed to be God's. I would say instead, give God what is divine and give science what is material. From that moment on, God does not and should not occur on scientific maps, since nature is not divine in itself—only its Maker is. Pope John Paul II was right when he said, "Scientific culture today requires Christians to have a mature faith."[22]

What had happened in the meantime is that the first scientists, later sanctioned by the Royal Society, had wisely and clearly demarcated their area of investigation. In their charter, King Charles II assigned to the fellows of the Society the privilege of enjoying intelligence and knowledge, but with the following important stipulation: "provided in matters of things philosophical, mathematical, and mechanical." That's how the "division of the estate" was executed. This partition led to a division of labor between the sciences and other fields of human interest. On the one hand, it gave to scientists all that could be solved by counting and measuring, so they were allowed to investigate what's in the Book of Nature. On the other hand, these scientists were told to avoid getting involved in all other domains— such as religion, education, legislation, justice, and ethics. In other words, these scientists agreed to limit themselves to questions that could be answered by material, physical, and mathematical means; all the rest was left for others to handle.

In this way, science bought its own territory at the expense of inclusiveness. From then on, all scientists kept profiting from this demarcation but, unfortunately, often forgot what it entails—limitation. For instance, the

---

22. "A Meditation from Pope John Paul II," in *Prayers and Devotions: 365 Daily Meditations,* ed. Peter van Lierde (New York: Penguin Books, 1998).

fact that God is missing on scientific maps does not mean in any way that science has replaced religion or is in competition with religion. God isn't measurable, countable, or quantifiable. Not everything that counts can be counted! Alas, many scientists have come to actually reject what they neglect—but luckily there are still many exceptions.

Many famous scientists were or are dedicated religious believers: legends like Johannes Kepler, Galileo Galilei, Blaise Pascal, Isaac Newton, Louis Pasteur, Antoine Lavoisier, Fr. Gregor Mendel, Lord Kelvin, Pierre Duhem, Michael Faraday, Alessandro Volta, James Maxwell, Fr. Georges Lemaître, and Max Planck, as well as more contemporary biologists such as Francisco Ayala, Francis Collins, Gerty Cori, Theodosius Dobzhansky, Kenneth Miller, and so many more. All these scientists uphold the religious conviction that God created the world according to an intelligible plan that is accessible to the human intellect through the natural light of reason. They all have in common a belief in a trustworthy Creator God who has actually made science possible. These scientists *trust* that nature is law-abiding and comprehensible in principle, which gives them reason to trust their reasoning.

I want to take this point one step farther: Creation may in fact be a much needed asset to science. Without the notion of the universe as a *created* entity, science would be a shaky and problematic enterprise. How could nature be intelligible if it were not created? How could there be order in this world if there were no orderly Creator? How could there be scientific laws if there were no rational Lawgiver? How could there be design in nature, if there were no intelligent Designer? How could there be human minds, if the universe were mindless?

To word these questions differently: Why is this universe law-abiding? Science has a fundamental "law" that declares everything is governed by laws of nature, but it cannot test this fundamental law the way it tests its later laws. Put more simply: How do we know there are laws in nature? Why do we expect the sun to rise every morning? Is the sunrise proof of a Creator God? No, it is not, but it certainly is a powerful *pointer* to a trustworthy Creator. How so?

Once we lose the notion of creation, plus the trustworthy order it comes with, scientific laws become very problematic. The philosopher David Hume and his followers headed down that blind alley. According to Hume, the law that the sun rises daily is merely a mental conception based on our habit of seeing the sun rise every morning. Indeed, that's the nonsense we are definitely in for once we disconnect science from creation. Once he made this assumption, Hume had no reason anymore to trust his own reasoning. He had lost sight of the fact that the laws of nature are a *given*, not an a priori or a posteriori thought pattern; they are to be discovered, not invented. If the laws of nature are just mental habits, it's hard to explain why bridges built in accordance with the physical laws and boundary conditions stand firm whereas others collapse. Would competent engineers really have better mental habits than their inept colleagues? There has got to be more to it! G. K. Chesterton once joked about a conspiracy of order in our world of regularity: "One elephant having a trunk was odd, but all elephants having trunks looked like a plot."[23] Well, science is in search of that plot! Clearly, science presupposes the existence of order. The philosopher John Stuart Mill inspired Darwin to say that it is a law that every event depends on a law—but he didn't say where he got that law from.

In the Judeo-Christian view, the universe is the creation of a rational Intellect that is capable of being rationally interrogated by all human beings, including the scientists among them. Without faith, reason loses its foundation—and so would science. Without God, we have no reason anymore to trust our reasoning.

Most people are aware that religion wouldn't do too well without science, but few realize the opposite—that science without religion wouldn't even be possible. Science was born in a Judeo-Christian cradle and would collapse as soon as this foundation were taken away. I believe it's quite evident that nature remains an enigma until nature is no longer ruled by whimsical deities, chaotic powers, or our own philosophical decrees and regulations. Once the Creator is Someone who can do whatever he likes, there is only one way to find out what God has actually done: Go out and look—in other words, you need to do experiments.

In this view, the universe is law-abiding and intelligible because it has been created by a lawful and rational God. This means that the universe is open to analysis and investigation by reason, for God could have created the world any way he liked. It shouldn't surprise us then that Copernicus could come up with the daring declaration that nothing would be easier for

---

23. G. K. Chesterton, *Orthodoxy* (New York: John Lane, 1908), 106–7.

God than to have the earth move, if he so wished. Here is that twosome of "faith and reason" again! In this sense, Francis Collins (the longtime leader of the Human Genome Project and a dear friend of Christianity) is right when he calls DNA "the language of God," because DNA, like anything else, does indeed follow God's laws. It is amazing that so many scientists have lost awareness of the very foundation of science, which is rooted in the concept of creation. Whether they like it or not, all scientists keep living off Judeo-Christian capital. God made very clear to Job that it was he who had "laid the foundation of the earth . . . [and] determined its measurements" (Job 38:4–5).

So it shouldn't surprise us that God has often been described as an Architect, an Artisan, or a Workman (*Deus Faber*). Relating to the Book of Wisdom (11:20), Pope Pius XI put it well: "The created world receives weight, number, and measure through the hands of God."[24] Even everything that can be counted comes from God. With God as the Architect, we are only minute builders and residents. In short, the ultimate source of intelligibility is a trustworthy Creator God who created the universe as an "intelligent project," in Pope Benedict's favorite terminology. It is in essence an intelligible plan accessible to the human intellect through the light of the reasoning mind. In chapter two, we discovered that the Biblical creation accounts share the same resounding message: It is the *order* of creation based on an intelligent, trustworthy design that frees the world from the caprice of chaotic, superstitious, and pagan powers. Genesis teaches us that the universe is not divine in itself but has been created by a divine rational intellect that is capable of being rationally interrogated. Cardinal Christoph Schönborn, OP, put it well when he said, "Nothing is intelligible—nothing can be grasped in its essence by our intellects—without first being ordered by a creative intellect."[25] Or to quote a famous scientist, the astrophysicist Sir James Jeans: "the universe begins to look more like a great thought than a great machine."[26] He essentially meant that physics is discovering more and more that the universe has an intrinsic rationality—I would say a cosmic order—that governs all that science is trying to decipher.

---

24. Pius XI, Address to the Plenary Session of the Academy: *The Complex Subject of Science Is the Reality of the Created Universe,* 1938.

25. Christoph Schönborn, "The Designs of Science," *First Things,* January 2006.

26. James Jeans, *The Mysterious Universe* (Edinburgh: Cambridge University Press, 1930), 139.

Ultimately, science and creation do make a good match—I would even say a match made in heaven. So why should we feel forced to make a choice between science and religion? This is a false dilemma. As the philosopher Peter Kreeft said, it's like an old Western in which one cowboy says to the other: "This town ain't big enough for both of us. One of us has to leave."[27] Why would one of them have to leave? They're not competing for a prize that only one can have; the loss of one would actually be the loss of both. Science without creation would be a blind alley, a stillbirth. And religion without science would be blind to many material aspects of the world. As Albert Einstein, a scientific authority, said, "Science without religion is lame, religion without science is blind."[28] Or as Pope John Paul II, a religious authority, said, "Science can purify religion from error and superstition. Religion can purify science from idolatry and false absolutes."[29] If you have the feeling that science is pulling you away from your faith, don't blame science—but maybe some particular scientists. And if you have the opposite feeling that faith pulls you away from science, don't blame your faith—but perhaps certain preachers.

In conclusion, the Book of Nature and the Book of Scripture complement each other as coming from the same source, God our Creator. Pope Benedict XVI likes to see "nature as a book whose author is God in the same way that Scripture has God as its author."[30] Or in the words of Saint Augustine: "It is the divine page that you must listen to; it is the book of the universe that you must observe."[31] As it turns out, science in itself is incomplete and religion on its own is insufficient. We can't live on bread alone, but neither can we live on faith alone. Reason requires faith (otherwise reason has no basis), and faith seeks understanding (otherwise faith becomes incoherent). We need to keep science and religion in balance; otherwise we will always remain unbalanced and lopsided as human beings. We need to put science in its place, but we also should put religion in its place, as the following chapters will show.

---

27. Peter Kreeft, "The Pillars of Unbelief," *The National Catholic Register* (Jan–Feb 1988).

28. *Science, Philosophy and Religion, A Symposium* (New York: The Conference on Science, Philosophy and Religion in Their Relation to the Democratic Way of Life, 1941).

29. Letter to the Rev. George V. Coyne, SJ, Director of the Vatican Observatory, June 1, 1988, in Robert J. Russell, *John Paul II on Science and Religion: Reflections on the New View from Rome* (Rome: Vatican Observatory Publications, 1990).

30. *Address to the Pontifical Academy of Science*, October 31, 2008.

31. *Enarrationes in Psalmos*, 45, 7.

=============== Delving Deeper ===============

## What Is a Species?

The concept of species is central to evolution. What binds the members of a species together? In short, what keeps a species together and what distinguishes it from other species? We need to answer these questions before beginning to discuss evolution.

It is tempting to consider a species as a group of similar-looking organisms. However, this is a very hazy conception: How similar is "similar," and where should we draw the line? Some people would prefer to adopt Wittgenstein's concept of "family resemblances."[32] Wittgenstein's point was that members of a family may have overlapping similarities, even if they don't have one essential feature in common.

In biology, however, the idea of overlapping similarities is still ambiguous. Most biologists have adopted a much more precise concept of species, which has been very successful among population biologists: the so-called biological (or reproductive) species concept. It was particularly developed and advocated by biologists such as Theodosius Dobzhansky (Columbia University), Francisco Ayala (University of California at Irvine), and Ernst Mayr (Harvard University), and it has been phrased in the following terms: Species are groups of interbreeding natural populations that are reproductively isolated from other such groups. According to this concept, a species is an evolutionary unit kept together by gene flow and isolated from other species by intrinsic isolating mechanisms of reproduction. Its members may share some similarities, but more importantly, they are isolated from other groups by reproductive barriers. So this concept of species is all about "family ties," and not so much "family resemblances." Similarities as such do not count for much, because they are merely a by-product of reproductive isolation; in theory, the members of a species could even have nothing in common but reproductive isolation.

The strength of this concept of biological species is that it relates our understanding of the concept of a species to our understanding of speciation processes. It offers an explanation of what maintains and what disrupts

---

32. Ludwig Wittgenstein (1953–2001), *Philosophical Investigations* (Malden, MA: Wiley-Blackwell, 1991), 66–71.

the unity of the species. To be more explicit, gene flow is the binding force behind a species, and at the same time it can be blocked through isolating mechanisms.

But what should we do with hybrids—crossbreeds between members of two different species (e.g. between horse and donkey, or between horse and zebra)? Are hybrids a problem for the biological species concept? Quite the contrary! Hybridization may still occur after two populations of the same species are separated and then come back into contact. If their reproductive isolation had had a chance to become complete, they would have already developed into two separate, incompatible species. If their reproductive isolation is not yet complete, then further mating between the populations will still produce hybrids, but these may not be fertile. Hybrids make sense when seen from an evolutionary viewpoint—but they wouldn't make sense if all species were created once and forever by the Creator. Keep in mind, before the rise of modern-day conservationists, most species didn't make it in evolution; they either became extinct or evolved into other species. It's estimated that 99.9 percent of all species that have ever lived no longer exist.

## The Mechanism of Speciation

Biologists have discovered many more cases to corroborate the claim that speciation does occur in nature, which is strong evidence for the synthetic evolutionary theory. But what is its underlying mechanism? First, speciation may be the result of doubling up all chromosomes, mostly in plants, thus isolating the offspring reproductively. Usually, however, speciation starts with some form of geographical isolation. After that, due to accumulating mutations, *geographical* barriers lead in time to *biological* barriers (such as differences in habitats, breeding times, mating rituals, sexual organ structures, infertility of hybrids, and incompatibility between sperm and egg). Take the two *Drosophila* species *pseudoobscura* and *persimilis;* they are very closely related, yet isolated from each other by habitat (*persimilis* generally lives in colder regions at higher altitudes), by the timing of their mating season (*persimilis* is more active in the morning and *pseudoobscura* at night), by behavior during mating (the females of both species prefer the males of their respective species), and by sterility of hybrid males. Even if the original barrier no longer exists, the new species may stay reproductively isolated due to its acquired biological barriers. Once geographical isolation has created reproductive isolation, speciation has become a fact.

On the other hand, not all geographical isolation is based on physical barriers such as mountains, deserts, or water (*allopatric* speciation). Other barriers exist, such as the mere physical *distance* between some members of a population. In such cases, the population is still continuous, but nonetheless, its members may not mate randomly; they are more likely to mate with their geographic neighbors than with individuals at a greater distance. This is called *parapatric* speciation. I like to compare this phenomenon with dialects spoken by human populations: Neighboring groups can easily understand one another, but they find it harder to understand people farther away because more changes in dialect occurred over longer distances. And isolation would further add to this growing apart (compare, for example, the English spoken in Australia, South Africa, and India).

How could such a parapatric situation lead to speciation? Consider the case in which the species forms a ring of neighboring populations; its members can interbreed with adjacent populations, but there may be at least two "end" populations in the series that are too distantly related to interbreed. An example is found in California, where the *Ensatina* salamander forms a horseshoe of populations in the mountains surrounding the Central Valley. Although interbreeding can happen between each of the nineteen populations around the horseshoe, the salamanders on the western end of the horseshoe cannot interbreed with the salamanders on the eastern end. The problem, then, is whether to classify the whole ring as a single species (although not all individuals can interbreed) or to consider each population as a separate species (although there is still interbreeding with nearby populations). This much is clear: If enough of the connecting populations within the ring perish to sever the breeding connection, the separated members would have become distinct species. It shouldn't surprise us, then, that, in an evolutionary context, what may seem like a clear-cut species concept inevitably becomes more fluid.

## Eating Away the Foundation of Science

There have always been, and will always be, scientists who think that the *meta*physical presuppositions of order, causality, and functionality are only *scientific*, empirical findings open to regular falsification—in mere ignorance of the fact that falsification wouldn't work without the assumption of order. Recently, for instance, many scientists developed a new interest in chaos and chaotic systems, as if these could ever falsify the existence of order. It's true that some natural systems can only be described by nonlinear mathematical equations with such complex solutions that we cannot exactly predict what the system will do in the near future. Or, to take another example, our measurements of all the initial conditions of a particular system (e.g. in meteorology) may be too numerous or too inaccurate to predict an exact outcome. However, the weather isn't really chaos—it only appears to be; as a matter of fact, we are looking for the order behind seemingly chaotic phenomena. When the weather forecast is wrong, does that mean the weather is unpredictable? Of course not; we just don't know enough to be perfectly accurate. And let's not forget that statistics—the science of randomness—is in itself a very orderly enterprise.

There was a passionate discussion in quantum physics between Albert Einstein and Niels Bohr. According to Heisenberg's principle of uncertainty or *indeterminacy*, it is impossible to determine simultaneously the values of position and momentum, or of energy and time, with any great degree of certainty; the more precisely one property is known, the less precisely the other can be known. The question is, though, how to interpret this phenomenon. In Bohr's interpretation (the principle of complementarity), these values are in essence undetermined until we measure one of them; light, for example, behaves either as a wave or a stream of particles depending on our experimental setup, but we can never observe both at the same time. Bohr's interpretation entails that the role of the observer is crucial in all of this; the measurement of position would necessarily disturb a particle's momentum, and vice versa; as a result, it is assumed these quantities have no precise values, so the behavior of atoms and electrons can no longer be predicted until measured. Einstein, on the other hand, always detested Bohr's interpretation. An electron's spin, for instance, only *appears* undefined, Einstein said, because some variables are still hidden and unknown. If this view is correct, uncertainty would not be located in the real world but in our *knowledge* of the real world.

Although I am not a physicist but a philosopher of science, I tend to side with Einstein, who would easily beat Bohr in his philosophical qualifications. (Bohr, however, conducted an effective PR campaign for his interpretation and developed a powerful school of fans, including Heisenberg). Besides Einstein, I prefer to join such giants as Max Planck, David Bohm, and Erwin Schrödinger who maintain that natural laws describe a reality independent of ourselves, whereas Bohr's interpretation means that we have lost contact with reality and causality, because we are supposedly dealing with mere appearances (such as Geiger counts). It's ironic that Bohr and his Copenhagen school try to give us a *causal* explanation of the alleged fact that *causal* explanations are impossible. They think that we *don't* know because we *can't* know. I would argue it's logically impossible to prove that something has *no* cause; causality can never be defeated conclusively by experiments, since causality is their very foundation. No wonder Einstein spent the last four decades of his life in a quest to restore *order* to physics. He realized that order does not come from science but enables science. Come what may, the indeterminacy debate is still alive in physics at the present time, and apparently . . . indeterminate.

Curiously enough, a similar debate is going on in the life sciences concerning the question: "Does each biological trait have a function, affecting survival and fertility?" At the macroscopic level, the situation seems rather straightforward, given that too many tonsils, adenoids, and thyroids were removed in past decades at a time when their functions were unknown. But at the molecular level, the situation looks more ambiguous: Is all genetic variability subject to selection? Some biologists have maintained that a lot of variability is "neutral," "random," "nonsense," or "nonfunctional" in terms of natural selection; some even speak of "random-walk" evolution, in their passion for randomness. What comes to mind is the issue of so-called junk DNA. Is this DNA really "junk," or would the adjectives "noncoding," "neutral," or "silent" be a better characterization? As explained earlier (3.1.6), repetitive DNA may very well function as a rich pool from which potentially advantageous new genes may emerge in evolution; if that's right, such DNA would not really be unused. And think of those micro-RNA genes that turned out to have a function no one had ever dreamed of. But even if some biologists maintain that certain DNA is in essence neutral or random, other biologists might counter that its function has not yet been found. One could even say that what seems "neutral" at this moment may well have positive selective value under future circumstances.

Again, it is logically impossible to prove that some specific biological feature does *not* have a function; functionality can never be conclusively ruled out. Of course, this is not to say that there is no place for randomness in evolution, but I think promoting "random-walk" evolution is often driven by an ideological obsession with randomness over order. In addition, we should always be aware that certain features may no longer have a function because of changing circumstances (think of rudimentary features: penguins still have wings but can no longer fly; bats still have eyes but can no longer see well) or that someday they may acquire a function again. Because natural selection is an interaction between design and environment, it selects the best design available, but always under volatile circumstances.

In conclusion, I would say that claims about intelligibility, order and causality, or design and functionality cannot be falsified or defeated—for the simple reason that they are not intrascientific statements, but rather extrascientific, metaphysical presuppositions that make science work the way it works. So no one could ever conclusively form a physical case that doesn't have a *cause*, or a biological case that doesn't have a *function*—for that would undermine the foundation of science. If someone does make such a claim, one could counter it with, "Keep searching for a cause or function that may be eluding you at this moment." We are dealing with protoscientific, metaphysical assumptions. Without them, science would crumble.

# CHAPTER 4

---◦◦×◦◦---

# Beware of Worldviews

## 4.1 The Case Against Evolutionism

A worldview allows for only one way of looking at the world—one exclusive, comprehensive, universal way. Monopolistic by nature, worldviews don't tolerate competitors. From this point on, I will use the ending "-ism" for any worldview or ideology based on a theory that originally covered a much narrower, more specific range of phenomena. *Evolutionism* is such a worldview. It pretends to have found a Grand Theory of Everything based on some evolutionary theory—usually in terms of natural selection. Being an ideology, evolutionism sees everything exclusively in the light of evolution, and therefore it regards any other worldview as a rival. It knows no bounds or fences. No wonder that evolutionism is hostile to religion, including its doctrine of creation. Evolutionism actually downgrades religion to the status of being itself the mere product of natural selection—and nothing more.

As the previous chapters attest, I accept evolution as a scientific fact. I also acknowledge evolutionary theory as an acceptable theory for the time being, since both evolution and evolutionary theory are backed by strong evidence. In that sense, Darwinism (or preferably neo-Darwinism) is not a worldview, but a neat bundle of scientific theories—which is not to say that we will never ever find any better alternatives in the future. However, the moment Darwinism changes evolution and its evolutionary theory into an ideology, it becomes *evolutionism*. I definitely do not agree with the totalitarian doctrine of evolutionism because of its dogmatic worldview pretensions, based on a belief in the omnicompetence of biology. Biology certainly is no know-all or cure-all. Students in our schools—from elementary school to university—deserve to be taught genuine science. They and their parents should not settle for some kind of ideology. But, in teaching the science of evolution and natural selection, we must also make clear its limitations—such is part of teaching genuine science as well. *Teach* it, don't *preach* it.

So what problems does evolutionism face? Let us discuss them in more detail.

## 1. Methodological limitations

Evolutionism is not aware of its inherent methodological limitations— or at least does not admit them. Whatever facts evolutionary theory may reveal about the role of accidental (or random) forces active in the evolutionary process, this leaves us only with a biological story and a biological point of view. The geneticist Theodosius Dobzhansky was wise to stress that in biology nothing makes sense except in the light of evolution.[1] But he knew well that there is more to life than biology (as the following chapters will highlight). Darwin may be to biology what Newton or Einstein is to physics, but we don't need to worship at Darwin's altar as evolutionism tends to do. Even science itself doesn't deserve a pedestal, as it is a very limited undertaking. Render to religion what is divine, but never render to science what is God's. We need not make biology a new religion; biology is not all-powerful or all-pervading—only God is. Good fences may make good neighbors, but evolutionists don't acknowledge any fences; they actually don't acknowledge any neighbors and try to silence religion. Evolutionism claims to have all the answers to all possible questions, including the answer that evolutionism is all there is and all that counts. They present this as a new kind of gospel, but it doesn't really sound like good news. And what gives them the certainty that only evolutionism is certain?

The evolutionist view regards everything in life outside this narrow scope as mere illusion. Evolutionism violates nearly all the "no-trespassing" signs set up in the previous chapter: It claims that science is final and

---

1. Theodosius Dobzhansky, "Biology, Molecular and Organismic," *American Zoologist*, vol. 4 (1964), pp. 443–452.

concerns the entire world and all its aspects, that it has a Grand Theory of Everything that can answer all our questions, that science is free of any metaphysical presuppositions or methodological limitations, and that it has replaced religion. However, all these claims are made from outside the scientific domain—which certainly takes the edge off their authority. So evolutionism has no logically compelling reasons for its claims.

Being an ideology, evolutionism is a dogmatic belief, a way of looking at the world that attempts to fit the world into an a priori idea. As a belief system, evolutionism demands adherence to the claims it puts forth. It claims to have effectively reduced teleology to mere causality in the form of natural selection, thus eliminating any annoying metaphysical questions. But as already noted, the causality of natural selection doesn't *explain* teleology but *assumes* it. It still leaves open such questions as "What is the selecting agent in the process of natural selection?" or "What it is that makes the design of the fittest so fitting and goal-directed?" The *cosmic* design determines which *biological* designs are possible, and then it filters those designs that fit best. The cosmic design contains the laws and constraints that regulate which biological designs "fit," and thus are successful in reproduction and survival. Next, we could very well claim that this cosmic design is the creative act of an Intelligent Designer. So it would indirectly and ultimately be the Creator who selects—the very Creator evolutionism claims to have effectively discarded.

## 2. Natural selection and the human mind

Another problem is that evolutionism works like a boomerang. The previous chapter discussed the paradox of self-reference: a theory such as the theory of natural selection cannot refer to itself—in other words, the theory of natural selection itself cannot be taken as a product of natural selection. This problem can easily be solved, however, by preventing the theory from becoming a "theory of everything" that would include itself.

But a much bigger and more serious problem arises here. Even if the theory of natural selection in itself is not the product of natural selection, it is still a product of the human mind (Darwin's, to be precise). And where does the human mind come from? Evolutionism says that the human mind is only a product of natural selection, for natural selection supposedly explains *everything* in life, including the human mind. But if that were really so, we would find ourselves trapped in a vicious circle. To his credit, Darwin himself was well aware of this thorny implication. He says in his *Autobiography* that if the theory of natural selection comes from the human mind, one might wonder whether "the mind of man, which has, as I fully believe, been developed from a mind as low as that possessed by the lowest animal, [can] be trusted when it draws such grand conclusions."[2] And in a letter, Darwin wrote: "With me, the horrid doubt always arises whether the convictions of man's mind, which has been developed from the mind of lower animals, are of any value or at all trustworthy. Would anyone trust in the convictions of a monkey's mind, if there are any convictions in such a mind?"[3]

Curiously enough, Darwin applied this doubt to one's belief in God, but not to his own belief in evolution. His conclusion was that we cannot trust anything we know about God, whereas I would argue the opposite—that we cannot trust anything we know at all if there is no God. Let me rephrase this thought in more revealing terms: If one doesn't trust the rationality of human beings, one is logically prevented from having confidence in one's own rational activities—with science being one of them. Evolutionism has run into trouble by cutting off its reason for reasoning! The problem would be solved if the human mind were not a product of natural selection—but that contradicts the universal claim of evolutionism. Once I take natural selection to be the only power shaping me and my mind the way it shapes my DNA, I would have reason to doubt what my rational capacities are really worth. And evolutionary theory fully depends on these very capacities, which gives it a rather shaky basis. If natural selection were the origin of all there is in life, including the human mind, it would act as a boomerang that comes back to its maker in a vicious circle, knocking out the truth claims of whoever launched it. A hand may draw a picture of itself, but a hand that draws a hand can never reproduce the same hand that does the drawing.

In short, how could we ever trust the outcome of mere natural selection when it comes to matters of truth? In fact, natural selection must *assume* the human mind, but it can neither create it nor explain it. On its own,

---

2. Charles Darwin, *The Autobiography of Charles Darwin*, ed. Nora Barlow (New York: Norton &and Company, 1958), 149.

3. Letter to W. Graham, 1881.

natural selection would be just a powerless and useless concept. As a matter of fact, the denial of God as our Creator is like an acid that eats away the foundation of rationality.

## 3. Restrictive claims

Evolutionism runs into a third problem. It acknowledges only physical causes and biological functions as being real factors operating in this world. Evolutionism is hard-core reductionism, touting nothing-buttery. As a result, evolutionism denies validity to other factors shaping our lives, such as motives, reasons, values, and destinations. However, neglecting those factors doesn't entitle one to deny or reject them. That would be akin to rejecting everything that cannot be tested with a thermometer!

One of the main reasons evolutionism makes this restrictive claim is that it enshrines the scientific method as the only way of finding truth. But this amounts to *scientism*—a baseless, unscientific claim made from outside the scientific realm, thus overstepping the boundaries of science. Let's take science off its pedestal and put it where it belongs. Never confuse a scientific map of the world with the world itself. Maps are only a surrogate for the real thing, so it won't do to replace the world with one of its maps.

Science itself can never prove it's the only way of finding truth; therefore, scientism is an ideology disguised as science. If someone says to you, "Let's play chess," and you ask, "Why?" then a question has arisen that the rules of chess are not framed to answer. Those rules cannot help determine if playing chess qualifies as a sport, or whether it's a worthwhile game; such issues lie outside their range. The same holds for the question of whether science is the only way of finding truth; this question comes from outside the scientific range.

In speaking about the world, however, we usually do distinguish more levels than causality and functionality, levels such as rationality and morality. A later chapter will discuss how "real" these latter levels are (5.1.), but for now I only want to stress that evolutionism is a very restricted outlook on life, like a severe case of tunnel vision. But isn't there more in life than what meets the eye? Scientists do restrict themselves to certain levels, but the claim that there are no other levels is an autocratic belief. I would counter: If evolutionism claims that most biological facts don't make sense without assuming evolution, religious faith has equal rights to claim that evolution doesn't make sense without assuming creation. *Neglecting* what is outside the scope of science may be a wise scientific strategy, but *rejecting* what is outside its scope goes one step farther and turns inevitably into a baseless, unjustifiable ideology.

Evolutionism reduces everything to purely material causes—which makes for a poor, barren kind of philosophy, as if science were the only way of understanding the real world. And that would confuse the scientific world with the real world. This ideology would destroy the human image. The things that count the most in life go beyond matter. As Shakespeare said, "there are more things in heaven and earth [ . . . ] than are dreamt of in your philosophy."[4] Pope Benedict XVI tried to widen the horizons of such a restricted outlook on life when he said:

> When men and women allow the magnificent order of the world and the splendor of human dignity to illumine their hearts, they discover that what is "reasonable" extends far beyond what mathematics can calculate, logic can deduce, and scientific experimentation can demonstrate; it includes the goodness and innate attractiveness of upright and ethical living made known to us in the very language of creation.[5]

Let's not forget that the astonishing successes of science have not been gained by answering every kind of question, but precisely by refusing to do so. Its success is bought at the cost of limiting its ambition, leaving a huge territory untouched. We may neglect—but cannot deny—what is beyond our horizon.

## 4. The concept of chance

This leads to a fourth problem with evolutionism. It adorns the scientific term *chance* as it is used in evolutionary theory with a capital C—the goddess of Chance, a sort of whimsical providence secretly worshiped and forcefully defended against rival deities, as one dogma against the other. It is true that evolutionary theory often speaks of randomness: mutations, environmental changes, and natural selection are all alleged to occur randomly. We can easily replace "randomly" with "by chance," because they are basically interchangeable. However, "chance" can carry many different

---

4. William Shakespeare, *Hamlet,* act I, scene 5.
5. Sermon during his pilgrimage to Cameroon, March 19, 2009.

meanings. Each time a biologist says that something happened "by chance," we should ask: How do you mean? Only then can we start a reasonable discussion.

The concept of chance (or randomness) in evolutionary theory never comes close to fate, destiny, doom, gloom, or meaninglessness. Yet some people, especially evolutionists, take the word "chance" out of its scientific context and interpret it as meaning "senseless" and "meaningless," which changes all of life into a mere play of whimsical, fortuitous events. By so doing, they have made Chance into a capricious, blind agent, actually a deity, or a "blind watchmaker" at best. So we end up with the deity of chaos versus the God of order. After that, they claim that evolution is a senseless and meaningless process—which is a dogmatic worldview again, disguised in the garment of science. Science has thus been turned into a pseudoreligion: omnipotent and omnipresent. One of its classical high priests was the paleontologist George Gaylord Simpson from Columbia University, who ventured to proclaim from his quasiscientific pulpit that "man is the result of a purposeless and natural process that did not have him in mind."[6] This view turns science into a pseudoreligion or monopolistic worldview. My response to Simpson's proclamation is actually very simple: Simpson says there is no God, and Simpson is his prophet!

Isn't it startling that evolution has produced some human beings who devote their entire career to the very *purpose* of proving that evolution has no *purpose* whatsoever? Or—to paraphrase one of C. S. Lewis' discoveries—if there were no light in the universe and therefore no creatures with eyes, we would never know it was dark.[7] Similarly, if there is no purpose in the universe, how could we ever know there is no such thing as purpose? In evolutionism, purpose is a forbidden idea in much the same way that freedom is in mechanicism. Put differently, how could human minds ever emerge from a mindless universe? Evolutionism is out to silence religion, but ultimately fails.

Please be aware that issues of sense, meaning, and purpose do not belong in scientific discourse—they cannot be featured on scientific maps, but are in the minds of mapmakers. Science may be everywhere, but science is not all there is. The question as to whether evolution has a meaning,

---

6. George Simpson, *The Meaning of Evolution* (New Haven: Yale University Press, 1967), 345.

7. C. S. Lewis, *Mere Christianity,* 3rd ed. (San Francisco: Harper, 2001), 46

destination, or purpose takes us into the domains of philosophy and religion. Science has no answers to these kinds of questions—no matter what evolutionism proclaims, or likes to proclaim. Science may claim that nothing in biology makes sense except in the light of evolution; philosophy, in turn, should argue that nothing in evolution makes sense except in the light of creation.

Seen from a *meta*physical viewpoint, there is nothing random in evolution. Human beings are *contingent:* that is, they could easily *not* have existed, since the reason for their existence can't be found within themselves. But that doesn't mean they are random or mere products of blind fate. They may have come *through* a process of evolution, but ultimately they must come *from* creation, or else they couldn't be here at all. In that sense, creation is a precondition for evolution—perhaps not a *logical* but a *rational* "must." True, evolution didn't have humanity "in mind"—for evolution itself is mindless—but it is the product of the Divine Mind of its Creator. Otherwise, we wouldn't and couldn't even be here.

## 5. Evolution cannot create order but must assume it

A fifth problem evolutionism faces is its typical yet wrong assumption that evolution can create order out of disorder—that is, out of the disorder of events happening "at random" or "by chance." It is true that evolution is a process in which the less complex may evolve into the more complex, but many evolutionists take it to be a process in which disorder evolves into order. First, the simple is in no way less orderly than the complex. A simple snowflake actually shows a very intricate order. Second, evolution cannot *create* order, but it must *assume* order. The physicist Stephen Hawking even went as far as saying that the universe created itself from nothing: "Because there is a law such as gravity, the universe can and will create itself from nothing. Spontaneous creation is the reason there is something rather than nothing, why the universe exists, why we exist."[8] But spontaneous creation is philosophical nonsense; for something to create itself, it would have to exist before it came into existence—which is impossible. Wouldn't it be nice if gold could create itself from nothing! It's plain truth that nothing

---

8. Stephen Hawking and Leonard Mlodinow, *The Grand Design* (New York: Bantam Books, 2010), 180.

comes from nothing. If gravity would be able to create the universe, wouldn't the law of gravity have to exist before there was gravity? Third, evolution may seem a disorderly process when taken in a purely scientific context; yet, evolution could never happen without the existence of order in the background. Let's not forget that DNA replication, reproduction, and natural selection are in essence orderly processes. Fourth, the study of evolution itself is certainly an intensely orderly enterprise—based on the assumption of *order* (as a precondition for confirmation and falsification), as well as on the assumption of *design* (as a precondition for natural selection). Natural selection actually follows the path of least resistance, which is determined by the cosmic design. How could chaos ever falsify the notion of order, given that falsification is impossible without the assumption of some cosmic order?

In addition, we have seen that evolutionism has made chance into a capricious, blind deity—the deity of chaos versus the God of order. However, chance itself can never create the order found in the living and nonliving world—as little as blindness can create sight. As the old saying goes, "what chance creates, chance destroys," because there is no purpose or direction to chance (just test it at a slot machine). It is the other way around: Chance is only intelligible in terms of the order which it *lacks*; a previous order must exist before any chance event can even occur. If there were no order, there could be no chance, because chance needs the order of preexisting causes coming together to produce unexpected results (which is called coincidence). Besides, what may seem random appears to be so by lack of sufficient knowledge; "orderless" phenomena might very well turn out to be extremely orderly if only we had more detailed and more accurate knowledge.

Yet, evolutionism insists that the world was built during evolution from the ground up—which means from chaos to order, or at least from simple to complex. True, evolution seems to have a time line that moves from less complex to more complex. But does this mean that the process of building more order is being steered by disorder? Atheists like Daniel Bennett think it is. Bennett says that religion has it wrong—"upside down" in his words— by claiming that God's creation *started* with order from the very beginning, whereas science places order at the *end* of an evolutionary process.[9] Is that

---

9. Michael Martin, ed., *The Cambridge Companion to Atheism* (New York: Cambridge University Press, 2007), chap. 8.

a checkmate? I don't think so. Although science tries to explain that order comes from *below*, religion keeps maintaining that order comes from *above*. As a matter of fact, the order we see in nature does not and cannot come from chaos, but it must come from a more fundamental order at a deeper level—which is the cosmic order of Creation governing everything that happens in the universe, including the process of evolution. The cosmic order regulates which processes are physically possible and which designs are biologically fit. Keep in mind that "law and order" are not a priori (rooted in the way we *think* about the world), but a given (rooted in the way the world *is*, having been created by a lawful God).

As science typically operates with a reductionistic, piecemeal approach, evolutionists would like to apply this to evolution by dissecting it into pieces—into changes on a gene-by-gene basis and selective processes on a step-by-step basis. Small wonder then that evolutionists mainly discover disorder in the process. However, their monopolistic worldview doesn't allow them to acknowledge the opposite approach—*meta*physical rather than physical—of putting things back together. This reversed approach would show that evolution has an underlying order of biological designs and genetic constraints—making the stream of evolution run in the bed of a cosmic design. There must be some form of underlying order, for no order could ever come forth from a purely chaotic universe—as little as human minds could arise in a mindless world, or moral values in an amoral universe. If the universe were only a collection of chance encounters, it would not be a rational universe, and therefore couldn't be rationally investigated, not even by science. Order is a "rational must" that is bound to come first so that it may carry the growing edifice of science.

## 6. The worldview claims of evolutionism

The sixth problem with evolutionism is that it offers us a baseless worldview, exclusively yet deceptively rooted in science—particularly in evolutionary science. I stress that science does not and cannot operate without the presuppositions of order and intelligibility, causality and regularity, functionality and design. Whether scientists accept this fact or simply ignore it, they have to live with it, perhaps reluctantly or even unknowingly and unwillingly, for science would collapse without those pillars. To paraphrase Ernst Von Brücke again, scientists treat them like a lady with whom they don't want to be seen in public but without whom they cannot live. These very presuppositions certainly did not originate from scientific research, but they are nevertheless the necessary basis for it; they need to come first before science can even begin. They are so implicit that they easily remain unnoticed, causing us to take them for granted.

But if science needs a foundation itself, how could it ever be, in and of itself, the foundation for a worldview? Yet, evolutionism presupposes that science is an enterprise completely sufficient on its own, and then makes it the basis for an all-pervasive, all-inclusive, monopolistic worldview. However, at the very moment we strip science from its roots and presuppositions, and then inflate it to a worldview, we can only find ourselves disillusioned with a baseless worldview, a phantom world floating like a castle about to vanish into thin air. Or, to use a different image, evolutionists have created their own swamp in which they are wading up to their knees. A worldview that portrays us solely as being a DNA chain produced by evolution is as fragile as the DNA structure that presumably generated this worldview; it cannot be worth more than its molecular origin. Basing its worldview exclusively on molecular structures, evolutionism rests on quicksand, as the foundation of science cannot be built on a foundation of molecules. Keep in mind that a worldview pretends to be all-inclusive—in this case, the only thing acceptable would be science; but if nothing outside science is permitted, we have cut off the very branch science sits on. So the dream of an all-knowing, all-powerful worldview based on sheer science is bound to be an illusion as well. It has lost its reason for reasoning and for trusting its own rationality.

## 7. The dangerous implications of evolutionism

My seventh and last objection to evolutionism concerns its potentially dangerous wider implications. If evolution based on natural selection is all there is to life, the future of humanity would forever remain "red in tooth and claw."[10] "Survival of the fittest" may work well in a scientific context, but that is not to say that it should exclusively rule all aspects of our lives as Spencer's dogmatic doctrine would have it. If it were the only guideline

---

10. Alfred, Lord Tennyson, *In Memoriam A. H. H.,* canto 56 (1850). The poem also contains the lines: "Are God and Nature then at strife / That Nature lends such evil dreams?"

in life, we would be bound for *eugenics*—the study and practice of selective breeding applied to humans, with the aim of actively improving the human gene pool.

The term *eugenics* was coined by Sir Francis Galton in 1883, drawing on the recent work of his half-cousin Charles Darwin. But it soon became a brutal movement that inflicted massive human rights violations on millions of people. The interventions advocated and practiced by eugenicists in Europe and the United States involved a wide range of people they deemed "degenerates" or "unfits"—the poor, the blind, the mentally ill, entire ethnic groups such as Jews, blacks, Roma (Gypsies), and the "dysgenic" victims of Margaret Sanger's *Planned Parenthood*; all of these were deemed "unfit" to live according to the eugenicists' despotic dogma of survival of the fittest. And this, in turn, led to practices such as segregation, sterilization, genocide, preemptive abortions, euthanasia, designer babies, and, in the extreme case of Nazi Germany, mass extermination. Forcing the weak to serve the strong is the cause of today's atrocities, but can easily become tomorrow's routine. Eugenics is essentially dedicated to the proposition that all people evolved unequally, which is perfectly in line with evolutionism. If natural selection is all there is, human beings can only *evolve* unequally, so they can only be *treated* accordingly as unequal, since they are not *created* equal. If humans are solely animals, we should be able to breed humans the way we breed animals. That's eugenics in a nutshell.

G. K. Chesterton was an early critic of the ideology of eugenics.[11] Eugenics wants the optimum in birth as opposed to the maximum in reproduction. Today's main critic is Pope Benedict XVI, who warned us of a new eugenics mentality. He condemned this "obsessive search for the 'perfect child,'" and added in response that "Man will always be greater than all that which makes up his body."[12] Just think of clergy and other celibate people who may hold back many "good genes" from future generations, but, unlike animals, have so many immaterial goods to offer to humanity. One of my professors once told me that Jesuits do a disservice to humanity by "withholding their high-quality genes," as he put it. When I answered him that they had so much more to offer than genes, he never mentioned it again.

---

11. Especially in his book *Eugenics and Other Evils* (New York: Cassell and Company, 1922).
12. In his *Address to the Pontifical Academy*, February 21, 2009.

Indeed, eugenics places the final end of human beings in their biological "worth," but Catholic teaching places it in eternal life. Put differently, the Church makes human culture subordinate to morality, whereas eugenics makes morality a mere product of human culture. Although eugenics did not develop from evolutionary theory itself, it is definitely an offshoot of evolutionism. In evolutionism, there is no good or bad. In regard to issues such as slavery, abortion, or genocide, evolutionism can only talk in terms of "winners" and "losers," because the concepts of "good" and "bad" are not only outside its scope but is even declared illusory. As Pope John Paul II observed, "When the sense of God is lost, there is also a tendency to lose the sense of man, of his dignity and life."[13]

Other objections could be made against evolutionism, but the seven objections put forth here provide enough evidence to discredit the sweeping claims of evolutionism. So we shouldn't be surprised that evolutionism has evoked a response—creationism.

## 4.2 The Case Against Creationism

Creationism is an entirely different worldview, the opposite of evolutionism; creationists are basically antievolutionists. Creationists don't just claim that God created the world (you and I do, too), but that he did so in a very human way by working miracles through a series of physical interventions at specific points in time. Apart from many, many differences among creationists, there is still a basic tenet in their "creation theory." It goes something like this. The earth and living things were created in six twenty-four-hour days some 6,000 to 10,000 years ago; some more "liberal" creationists treat these "days" as six separate, but much longer periods of time. Since the creative acts were miraculous events, they presumably do not fit within the framework of natural mechanisms as we know them. "In the beginning," God created some basic types, which were living together in harmony (that is, without bloodshed); hence, fossilization did not take place in those days. Different ecosystems existed next to one another—for example a Devonian landscape bordering a Cretaceous sea. A protecting and bracing atmosphere created a kind of greenhouse, thus allowing for more and bigger organisms than we see nowadays. One of the

---

13. *Evangelium Vitae*, no. 2.

consequences is, of course, that humans and dinosaurs must have coexisted. If science seems to tell us a different story, most creationists will point out that God intentionally designed these so-called scientific facts to trick us, and to test our faith.

Being an ideology, creationism claims a monopoly status as a comprehensive, dogmatic doctrine. Hence, creationists force you to make a choice in favor of creation the way they understand it—and consequently, against evolution. Whereas evolutionism is a case of science trying to silence religion, creationism is a case of religion attempting to silence science.

I don't like the idea of trading one worldview for another one; in this case, a creationism that rejects science and makes a pseudoscience out of religion. Yet, I am sympathetic to the cause of creationists, because they too are fighting a battle against the evolutionist ideology of atheists such as Richard Dawkins, Daniel Dennett, E. O. Wilson, Francis Crick, and Peter Singer, who attack religion and abuse science to advance their own ideological agenda. But first I wish to analyze whether creationists use the right weapon to combat the atheism of evolutionists who are out to destroy the human image.

Creationists tend to go overboard and reject any form of evolution; basically, they even reject most forms of science (including such tools as the radioactive dating of rocks). To word this more carefully: They usually maintain that scientific evidence, if there is such a thing, actually disproves evolution and supports their own literal interpretation of the biblical creation accounts. That's why they are called fundamentalists.

In general, most creationists are concentrated in the United States and Australia. They are mainly evangelical or fundamentalist Protestants, with only a few Catholics in the mix. The following points sketch the basic tenets of creationism:

&#10070; Some creationists maintain that evolutionary theory is not a science at all, but only some kind of secular religion. They are right when it comes to evolutionism, but as I showed earlier, evolutionary theory is fundamentally different from evolutionism and *does* qualify as a scientific theory. Nevertheless, in order to discredit the life sciences, creationists scan scientific literature for controversies and dissident views, not realizing that disputes and disagreements are at the heart of science and make it advance.

❖ Other creationists claim that evolutionary theory can never be put to the test, because it would be compatible with anything and adaptable to any circumstances. I argued before that the evolutionary theory is definitely falsifiable. Even the theory of common descent would be falsified, for example, if apes didn't have DNA more similar to ours than to other mammals, or if we would ever find a fossil rabbit in layers from the Precambrian era (3.4.).

❖ Creationists argue that randomness could never create something as intricate as life based on "lifeless" molecules. However, they misinterpret randomness and wrongly compare such a process with a chimp creating *Hamlet* on a typewriter by randomly hitting keys.

❖ Some creationists consider evolutionary theory basically a tautology, and thus meaningless—something like: "Who survive? The fittest! Who are the fittest? Those who survive!" In coming to this conclusion they have mixed things up, because biological fitness actually has a double meaning: It refers to the role of an organism as the subject (or cause) of reproduction, but also to the role of an organism as the object (or effect) of reproduction. This ambiguity also affects the fitness concept: It can refer to *potential* reproductive success (a cause), or to *actual* reproductive success (an effect). The slogan "survival of the fittest" is not a tautology if we take fitness as potential reproductive success, or reproductive capacity. The principle of natural selection (or survival of the fittest) asserts that organisms that are *potentially* successful in reproduction are more likely to be also *actually* successful in reproduction. Having a good design does matter in evolution, although additional factors are involved, such as migration, nurture, catastrophes, and so forth.

❖ All creationists probably do agree that Darwinism is an atheistic enterprise. It depends on what they mean by this statement, though. If they reject the theory because it doesn't mention God, I have to point out again that God does not, cannot, and should not occur on scientific maps. If they mean that the theory was discovered—or probably invented, in their view—by an atheist, I would say that's not a good reason to reject it, even if this accusation were true. The fact that the physicist Marie Curie was an agnostic doesn't affect her discovery of radioactivity. However, creationists may reject Darwinism because they think it made Darwin turn from a religious believer into an atheist. Quite some controversy exists on this point, however. It is true that Darwin did take the Bible quite literally until he joined the *Beagle*. After his trip, he became more of a deist than a theist. But even if he did become an atheist, this may have happened *after* he developed his theory, but not necessarily *because* of his theory. He himself said that the devastating loss of his ten-year-old daughter, Annie, made him an agnostic (a word that Thomas H. Huxley had invented; Lenin later called it a "fig-leaf" for materialism). As early as 1868 (only nine years after Darwin's famous publication), Blessed John Henry Cardinal Newman wrote in one of his letters, "Mr. Darwin's theory need not then be atheistical, be it true or not; it may simply be suggesting a larger idea of Divine Prescience and Skill."[14] Those words came from a very clear and wise Catholic mind.

Although I respect some of the creationists' intentions, I also have many serious objections against their approach. Fortunately, I am in good company, since Pope Benedict XVI has warned us against the way creationism reads the Bible. In July 2007, the pontiff discussed the debate raging in some countries between creationism and evolution, saying, "This antithesis is absurd." Yes, he actually said it is *absurd* to think that "those who believe in the Creator would not be able to conceive of evolution, and those who instead support evolution would have to exclude God."[15] I couldn't agree more. The good news is that Jesus was not a fundamentalist either.

So what is the problem with creationism? The following points indicate several serious objections to it.

## 1. *The text of Genesis*

First, creationism focuses heavily on Genesis 1, while ignoring its differences with Genesis 2. It takes the fundamentalist position that the first chapters of Genesis are literal accounts—written by "reporters" with a "scientific" agenda. But creationists should at least clarify why they have chosen

---

14. Letter to J. Walker of Scarborough, May 22, 1868, *The Letters and Diaries of John Henry Newman* (Oxford: Clarendon Press, 1973).

15. Benedict XVI, Meeting with the Clergy, July 24, 2007, see http://www.vatican.va/holy_father/ benedict_xvi/speeches/2007/july/documents/hf_ben-xvi_spe_20070724_clero-cadore_en.html.

the seven-day account of Genesis 1 over the dayless account of Genesis 2. Some creationists claim that Genesis 1 was written "from God's perspective," whereas Genesis 2 was written "from Adam's perspective." However, this doesn't explain the serious inconsistencies between the two chapters. Although chapters 1 and 2 do report the story of creation, Genesis does not present a step-by-step description of the initial stages of this world. For example, there is the problem as to how God could create light and even plants before creating the sun. But Genesis is not interested in this aspect; instead, it relates to us where this world really comes from (see number 5 below).

As shown earlier (2.3), according to Genesis, God's creation is not a scenario of creative interventions and historical milestones, but a continuing, enduring act of love! Yet, creationists keep claiming that the Book of Scripture should be read as if it were the Book of Nature. But it seems quite obvious that Genesis is not concerned with whether humanity was created *before* all plants and animals (Gen 2:7) or *after* (Gen 1:26). It could have been by a process of evolution . . . Is coming forth from the animal world really more belittling than coming from the dust of the earth?

Also, to mention only one of the many problematic details, creationists give a *biological* interpretation to the verses that say God created all creatures according to their kinds (cf. Gen 1:12; 1:21). So they assume that God "must" have created all species once and forever. However, we can't read Genesis as if it were a textbook on biology; it does not pretend to explain the *biological* version of the species concept. Instead, it is more about *kinds* than *species*; therefore, its classification is more practical than biological (distinguishing swimming creatures and winged birds in 1:21, and cattle, creeping things, and wild animals in 1:24). We may wonder what makes cattle qualify as a separate kind. Later, the Bible even gives a *theological* classification (e.g., water creatures with or without fins and scales, land animals with or without cloven hooves [cf. Deut 14]—that is, kosher kinds vs. nonkosher kinds). If Genesis were really about biology, why would God create so many varieties of certain kinds of animals? The biologist John Haldane said, "The Creator would appear as endowed with a passion for stars, on the one hand, and for beetles on the other, for the simple reason that there are nearly 300,000 species of beetle known."[16]

---

16. John Haldane, *What Is Life? The Layman's View of Nature* (London, Alcuin Press, 1949), 248.

And when calling a mustard seed the smallest of all seeds (cf. Mt 13:31, Mk 4:30, Lk 13:18), Jesus is not teaching us botany, for botany knows of even smaller seeds (e.g., orchid seeds).

Besides, Genesis does not present a biological taxonomy. Birds and fish were created on the fifth day in order to "adorn" the firmament and waters separated on the second day, whereas the land animals were created on the sixth day after the land and its vegetation had been separated from the water on the third day. Seen from a *biological* point of view, a taxonomy like this wouldn't make much sense; there is obviously a *theological* message here.

But there is more. If we would follow creationists and take Genesis 1 as a biological exposé on the origin of species, we would run into trouble as soon as we want to explain hybrids in nature. In a world of fixed species, there is no place for hybrids such as mules. In biology, on the other hand, hybrids are only an indication that the speciation process has not yet been finalized. The fact that horses and donkeys can still interbreed strongly indicates common descent. Of course, creationists could counter that horses, donkeys, and mules must belong to the same "species" or kind, but such a move would require enormous mental acrobatics. Instead, creationists ought not to read the Book of Scripture as if it were the Book of Nature.

## 2. Methodological problems

Second, creationism violates some basic methodological rules that are an integral part of all empirical sciences. Although some followers like to rephrase creationism as "creation science," they are rather hostile to science and its methods. In particular, fans of the so-called *Young Earth Creationism* (YEC) argue that the earth must be less than ten thousand years old (not all creationists agree, though), and that evolution is a lie. According to this argument, all the things science has come up with—such as the radioactive dating of rocks, all the fossils that were unearthed, and all the similarities and dissimilarities in DNA sequences we have found—were intentionally designed by God to test our faith, so it would look as if the universe were old, whereas in fact it is not. Others are more careful and assert that these deceptions come from Satan. In either case, we would be dealing with fake evidence made to fool us. First, such a claim amounts to some kind of conspiracy theory—an unbeatable theory, so to speak, because it is a theory that doesn't allow for falsification. In addition, scientific theories should not only explain but also predict, but predictions are totally missing here. Ideally, a scientific theory should not leave much wiggle room to tweak the theory.

Nevertheless, this theory leads to a much bigger problem: If creationism were true, God would have had to engage in massive deception, and science would be dealing with nothing more than fabricated objects. So we end up with intellectual suicide and, even worse, with a caricature of God. Science works with laws, which somehow do God's work. God doesn't have to keep the planets moving or to make species evolving. His creation keeps those laws in effect. Evolution is God's way of creating. God does not make things himself, but he makes sure they are made.

The biologist Kenneth Miller from Brown University likes to tell the story of how he detected that two of his students had submitted the same paper. They denied the charge, of course, since they had changed some details and had moved paragraphs around. So how could their professor have detected the fraud? He ran both papers through a program that looks for unusual matching strings and found six words misspelled in the same way. Just like spelling errors point to a common original text that was copied, genetic errors point to common ancestry. I don't see another explanation, unless we go for the unbeatable theory that God or Satan made them appear this way.

Creationists basically distrust science, even to the point of hating it, or at least they want to strictly censor its outcome. They may permit biologists to study all species individually, but transitions between them (speciation) are off limits. This is like telling physicists that they are allowed to study the individual elements of the periodic system, but they should never touch transitions between the elements (radioactivity). My advice to creationists would be: Don't fight science, for that's a hopeless battle; use your energy instead to fight *scientism*, for that's a battle you can win.

## 3. Cases of flawed design

Third, creationism ignores cases of "flawed design" in creation—cases that are hard to reconcile with a creative intervention of a loving God. A benign God would not include design flaws that lead to pain or unnecessary death, such as our appendix, our overly crowded jaws, or the birth of babies through the pelvis. From an evolutionary perspective, however, these cases do make sense.

The appendix is the remnant of an organ that was functional when our ancestors were still herbivores. And our jaws, which do not protrude as much as they did in our ancestry, have become overly crowded. This often leaves no room for the third molars (wisdom teeth). And because the human birth canal passes through the pelvis, a structure inherited from our ancestors, the baby cannot be born naturally if the baby's head is significantly larger than the pelvic opening (calling for a caesarean section). Or take the case of the human male, whose testes develop initially within the abdomen (an ancestral feature dating back to cold-blooded animals). Later, during gestation (although sometimes delayed), the testes migrate through the abdominal wall into the scrotum (as is typical for warm-blooded animals.) This process causes two weak points in the abdominal wall where hernias can later easily form.

All these cases make sense if we consider them to be evolutionary compromises. But how would creationism deal with these facts? Many creationists would respond that if it's good design, God did it, but if it's deficient design, it's a result of the Fall—after which God said to Eve: "I will greatly increase your pangs in childbearing" (Gen 3:16). In science, however, such a response violates basic methodological rules by introducing unscientific principles, making theories unbeatable and irrefutable. Theories that explain everything or predict anything actually explain nothing and predict nothing, because they act like a constantly moving target, hard to hit.

The creationists' maneuver of adducing the Fall as an explanation for what is "wrong" in nature has another problem, which Saint Thomas Aquinas points out: "Some say that the animals, which are wild now and kill other animals, were not that way [in paradise . . . ]. But this is entirely unreasonable. The nature of animals was not changed by the sin of man."[17] Of course, it's not easy to solve the problem of physical evil, and that is not the focus of this book, but to quote Aquinas again: "If all evil would be banned, the universe would lack much good. If it couldn't kill animals, the lion would not be able to live."[18] His point is that physical evil may sometimes serve a higher good (but there's more to that discussion).

---

17. *Summa Theologica* I, 96, 1, 2.
18. Ibid. (I, 22, 2, 2).

## 4. The difference between causes and grounds

Fourth, creationism mixes up causes, functions, and grounds, dumping them all in the same bag. Creationism does not recognize, let alone accept, that the doctrine of creation is about the "whys" or the *grounds* of life, and that the theory of evolution, on the other hand, is about the "hows" or the natural, physical *causes* of life. Creationism may solve why-problems, but it cannot solve how-problems in the way science does. So it comes up with *how* answers to otherwise legitimate *why* questions. This procedure is confusing, uncalled for, and even illegitimate. To put it in more general terms, religion and philosophy tell us *that* God creates the world, whereas science tells us *how* he does it. The question *"Why* did life arise?" is very different from and yet just as important as, if not more so, the question: *"How* did life arise?" These two questions must not be mixed up! Science may look for causal mechanisms, but philosophy and religion tell us where these mechanisms ultimately come from.

Saint Thomas Aquinas uses a terminology slightly different from mine; he speaks of *primary* and *secondary* causes. Thus he makes exceptionally clear the following important distinction: Regular, *physical* causality reigns inside the universe, linking causes together in a chain of (secondary) causes. *Creational* causality, on the other hand, reigns outside the universe as a Primary Cause, thus providing, so to speak, a point of suspension for the chain itself. As a consequence, creation has its own (metaphysical and/or religious) account, as distinct from other accounts (including scientific accounts). Aquinas didn't know about evolution, of course, but if he had, he would probably have said that evolution offers us a *scientific* account of how a later state of the material world might have emerged from an earlier state—whereas creation offers a *metaphysical* account of where the material world itself comes from.

In other words, the concept of creation doesn't even touch on what was the initial state of the material world. Sadly, this distinction between creation and evolution has been completely lost on creationists. There is no need to be so afraid of science, for scientists only try to *explain* this world; they could never *create* this world. Even if the Big Bang marked the beginning of this universe, it's still God who created all of it. Without creation, there could be no evolution. The Primary Cause lets the secondary causes do their work—or vice versa: the secondary causes can do their work thanks to the Primary Cause.

Perhaps the distinction between origin (primary cause) and cause (secondary cause) could be clarified by applying it to the comparable concepts of creation and *pro*creation. Procreation is based on physical causes and biological functions, which is the domain of science. Creation, on the other hand, is based on grounds, purposes, origins, and destinations, which is the domain of philosophy and religion. Thanks to this distinction, my parents can be seen as the natural *cause* of my being here, but God is the transcendent *ground* of my being in existence and alive. Understood this way, children come *through* us but not *from* us. God is not in a competition with our parents. God is not competing with our evolutionary ancestors either. We are just God's creatures, and creatures are not next to God or outside God, but they are in God. Outside God, there is nothing. Saint Paul said, "in him we live and move and have our being" (Acts 17:28).

In a similar way, medication may be the natural *cause* of my healing, but this doesn't detract from God as the *source* of my healing. Healing comes *through* but not *from* medication. No competition is going on between God and my parents, between God and my ancestors, or between God and my doctor. This is not a competition for a prize that would be lost by one if it were won by the other; there isn't just one winner. We should not mix them up, nor turn religion into a pseudoscience, or science into a semireligion. Put differently, we shouldn't give religious answers to scientific questions, or scientific answers to religious questions.

## 5. Creation differs from chronology

Fifth, creationism treats creation as a chronological scenario, a series of events that occurred long ago, on seven consecutive days of the very first week of the world's calendar. Is creation really a series of events, or even a one-time event? Saint Thomas Aquinas has some great thoughts on this issue. When he calls God the "First Cause," he is not thinking in terms of time, except for the fact that the universe may have a beginning. "First" should be understood as first in rank, not in time. This so-called First Cause is primarily the *fundamental* cause of this world—the ground and origin of all that is, seen and unseen. Creation means first and foremost that the world is *contingent*—dependent on its Creator for its existence. So God as Creator is not just Someone who did something at some time in the past, he is Someone who does something at all times. God keeps the world in existence (Saint Thomas calls this more specifically *preservation* or *conservation*). If the Creator's support were to be withdrawn at any time, the whole universe would simply collapse into nonexistence. In Aquinas' view, preservation is no different from creation; they both depend on God.[19] Since the world completely depends on God, it does so now, in the past, and in the future. Evolution or not, the world depends completely on God, for without God the world would be nothing. A world in evolution depends on God just as much as would a static world.

But there is more. Aquinas is actually denying that creation is some chronological episode, located somewhere back in time, when he says, "God brought into being both the creature and time together,"[20] and "Before the world, there was not time."[21] The world may have a beginning and a timeline, but creation itself doesn't have a beginning or a timeline; creation actually makes the beginning of the world and its timeline possible. Creation creates chronology, but it cannot become part of chronology, nor can chronology be the framework in which creation operates. The first chapters of this book have shown that a *chronological* interpretation of Genesis 1 doesn't work. God created time, but he certainly doesn't need time for his creation (not even a week); creation actually creates time.

So while creation does not explain the initial stages of this world, it does explain how any stages of this world could have come into existence. Creation isn't a trigger event like the Big Bang; actually it isn't an event at all. On the contrary, creation must come first before any events can follow, even a Big Bang. In other words, creation is not about the *beginning* of this world, but about the *origin* of this world (including its beginning and all its subsequent stages). The rest of the story would be something for science and evolution to tell. Pope Benedict XVI stressed this same point: "Thomas observed that creation is neither a movement nor a mutation. It is instead the foundational and continuing relationship that links the creature to the Creator, for he is the cause of every being and all becoming (cf. *Summa Theologica*, I, 45, 3)."[22]

---

19. *De Potentia Dei*, 5, 1, 2
20. *Contra Gentiles*, II, 32
21. *De Potentia Dei*, 3, 2
22. Address to the Pontifical Academy of Sciences, 2008.

In speaking of God as the First Cause, Aquinas put forth God as the first uncaused cause of existence, on Whom the universe depends perpetually and permanently for its very existence. Creation is not a one-time event, a series of events, or even a moment in time, but the origin of time—and hence, of everything else. In other words, creation is not a step-by-step scenario of creative acts, in the way creationists like to see it. "*In* the beginning" should be understood not in a temporal or chronological sense, but in a transcending sense, more in the sense of "originally" (*before* any beginning) than "initially" (*at* the beginning). Everything that exists depends on the Creator; he is the origin and beginning of everything. We are God's creatures, and creatures are not next to God or outside God, they are only and necessarily in God. Through him, with him, and in him, we live and move and have our being. Outside God, there is nothing.

## 6. God as the First Cause

Sixth, creationism disrupts the delicate balance between God's transcendence and God's immanence. If God is the First Cause—that is, the ground and origin of our existence—then he cannot be the (secondary) cause of my existence at the same time. The secondary cause of my existence is to be found in my parents and their evolutionary ancestors, but God is the primary cause or ground of my existence. In other words, when looking for material causes, we do not need to bring in God as a secondary, intervening cause as creationism does. That would amount to reducing God's transcendence to an innerworldly, physical cause. God is never a secondary causal link or switch in all world events, but he is their transcending origin and destination. God is not the One to physically keep the planets going, but he lets his physical laws do that. Again, we should avoid reading the Book of Scripture as if it were the Book of Nature.

Saint Thomas helps us make some clear distinctions here when he distinguishes creating (*creare*) from producing (*facere*).[23] The Creator creates the world, which means that he makes something from *nothing*. The potter, on the other hand, produces a pot, which means he makes something from *something* else. The universe may have been *produced* by the Big

---

23. *De Symbolo Apostolorum*, 33.

Bang, but it was *created* by God. In other words, creation is something completely unique; only God can *create*—that is, bring something into existence that didn't exist in any way before. Evolution, instead, is not a process of creating something from nothing, but of producing something from something else.

The Designer is immanent in every single detail of what he designed, yet he is not a part of it but is transcendent to it all. C. S. Lewis noted that a power outside the universe "could not show itself to us as one of the facts inside the universe."[24] God as the Architect of the universe is not a subsidiary part or element of what he designed; he is not a Divine Foot in the door. God can never act like an element or a part of his own creation, just as architects and engineers cannot be a part of the structures they build, even as they are part of every part. If there is a missing link in our scientific, causal explanation of the world, such a link can never be God. God is not a response to our scientific needs; instead, his laws take care of those needs. God is the *source* of all being, not a super-being among other beings, acting like them.

That is why science can never "bump into" God—not because science denies God (it doesn't or at least shouldn't), but because God is outside its framework and therefore cannot be a subordinate part of it. The moment we treat God as a causal link, in order to explain the gaps in our current scientific knowledge, we make him a "God of the Gaps"—of scientific gaps, that is, which doesn't negate God's ability to intervene with genuine miracles. When the frontiers of science are being pushed farther and farther back (which is bound to happen), then God is being pushed back with them as well. God should never be the victim of scientific expansion, nor should he be at the mercy of scientists. A God of the Gaps would be a *secondary* cause in his own creation—some kind of missing link in a cascade of causes. As the theologian Dietrich Bonhoeffer famously put it, "We are to find God in what we know, not in what we don't know."[25] Thank God and his Church for giving us the twosome of faith and reason.

In view of all this, my advice to creationists would be: Don't fight evolution, but do fight evolutionism, for that's a battle you can win, and it is one that's absolutely worth winning.

---

24. *Mere Christianity*, Book 1, p. 21

25. Dietrich Bonhoeffer in a 1944 letter: *Letters and Papers from Prison*, ed. Eberhard Bethge, trans. Reginald H. Fuller (New York: Touchstone, 1971).

## 7. Creationism is a worldview

Seventh, creationism offers only a new dictatorial worldview, one based on creation alone. Since all ideologies claim a monopoly, they leave no middle ground and force you to take sides: in this case, either God or nature. It's not fair to reject science, yet use its achievements when they benefit our lifestyle and medical well-being. But creationism claims that creation—or "creation theory" for some—provides us with a pervasive, exclusive, and universal explanation of life, without regard for almost any scientific facts. So it's not surprising that creationists have been demanding equal time for evolutionism and creationism in the science curriculum of our schools. But because these two are rival ideologies, they cannot occupy the same arena. If one is true, the other one must be false. Creationism claims a monopoly without tolerating any competition, thus silencing science, which is basically another form of megalomania—a quirk of our own making. As a result, many creationists consider all scientists atheists. However, if they sentence all scientists as a group, then they can't blame evolutionists for attacking all the faithful collectively.

Consider the following analogy. Creationists tell us we have only *one* choice, so we must decide whether the Grand Canyon was carved out by God or by the Colorado River—and you'd better opt for God. But that's not the dilemma we are facing here. The Grand Canyon was *made* by river streams yet *created* by God. Please don't force me to choose! Science and religion are not competitors; they are neighbors, each one with their own domain, perspective, and authority. So each offers a one-sided story, but cannot deny the other side. Creation is *not* about explaining physical things (as evolution is), but about explaining *why* there are any physical things at all (which is a *meta*physical or religious issue).

To conclude: I am sympathetic to the cause of creationists because they are fighting a battle against the evolutionist doctrines of atheistic scientists who abuse science for their personal agenda. However, creationists mistakenly consider all scientists to be evolutionists, and therefore atheists. Once they make such a move, they cannot blame evolutionists for regarding all religious believers as creationists, and therefore eccentric fundamentalists. Besides, creationists read the Book of Scripture as if it were the Book of Nature. If any fundamentalists, whether Christian or Muslim, were allowed to stifle science, scientists would not be allowed to study the Book of

Nature. But we shouldn't be forced to vote on whether the Grand Canyon was carved out by God himself or by the Colorado River. Pope Benedict XVI would respond, "this contrast is an absurdity!"[26] Or, as the *Catechism* puts it concisely, ". . . methodical research . . . can never conflict with the faith."[27] Creationists need to put religion in its proper place, just as evolutionists need to put science in its proper place.

## 4.3 The Impossible Dream: Intelligent Design Theory

Some people argue (but it's hard to prove) that the theory of *Intelligent Design* (ID) is a revamped form of creationism, redesigned when creationism could not make it into the school system. I fully understand why creationism did not make it, because it had so many antiscience elements that it could not successfully compete with evolutionary theory in schools. The theory of ID, on the other hand, seems to have a better chance, because it appears to be more seriously crafted. But let me stress first that the theory of ID is not a narrow worldview or ideology in the way evolutionism or creationism is. That may be another reason why it may have a better chance in the school system.

What is Intelligent Design? Proponents of ID—including both Protestants and Catholics (with authors such as Michael Behe, William Dembski, Michael Denton, Phillip E. Johnson, and Stephen C. Meyer)—claim that science itself can discern a Designer. They are often cool, if not hostile, to the theory of evolution, but they don't want to be called creationists. The Creator, or Designer of Life, in their view, can't be scientifically specified as God, but neither can God be ruled out. Most of them argue that no natural process can account for the complexity of nature (including the emergence of human beings), and that therefore we must invoke supernatural interventions by a Designer at several stages in the evolutionary process. This all sounds very reasonable, doesn't it?

Let's analyze the concepts behind ID. There is some discord among ID theorists, which is okay, as long as they don't use any disagreement among their opponents as an argument against them, but a common tenet is their focus on "irreducible complexity" in nature. ID theorists want to bring to

---

26. Benedict XVI, Meeting with the clergy, July 26, 2007.
27. CCC, no. 159.

our attention the perceived failings of evolutionary theory to account for life's subsequent stunning complexity—and that's where their plea for an intervening Designer comes in. Francis Collins—a longtime leader of the Human Genome Project, a dedicated Christian but an ID skeptic—likes to describe the main intentions of ID fans in this somewhat disrespectful, yet accurate way: "When science needs divine help."

The idea that complexity requires a designer is certainly not new. The Roman philosopher Cicero introduced this idea around 50 b.c.: "When you see a sundial or a water clock, you see that it tells the time by design and not by chance. How then can you imagine that the universe as a whole is devoid of purpose and intelligence?"[28] In the early nineteenth century, William Paley's watchmaker analogy was widespread: A watch is so complex that it must have had a maker, and since life is much more complex, it must have had a maker as well. Even Darwin himself, before his voyage on the *HMS Beagle*, was convinced of this idea—but his findings on the Galapagos Islands made him change his approach.

More recently, ID advocates have shifted their attention to complexities found in cell biology—in particular the intricacies of the molecular machineries in the cell. They question whether such complex machinery could have ever arisen only from mutation and natural selection. The question is certainly not new. We have already discussed that evolutionary biology has to assume (perhaps reluctantly or even unknowingly) the notion of preexisting design, but then would explain concrete, specific cases of biological design in terms of natural selection based on mutations. Yet, ID would go one step farther: Complexity can only be produced by a Designer's *intervention*—an intelligent, supernatural cause—in addition to or instead of the natural processes of mutation and natural selection. Let's see which side to take in this debate:

One of the classic examples used by ID supporters is the bacterial flagellum, a whiplike appendage that, like an outboard motor, propels bacterial cells in various directions. It does indeed show quite impressive complexity. DNA expert Francis Collins describes it this way:

> The structure of the flagellum, which consists of about thirty different proteins, is really quite elegant. It includes miniature versions of a base anchor, a drive shaft, and a universal joint. All of this drives a filament propeller.

---

28. *De Natura Deorum*, ii. 34

The whole arrangement is a nanotechnology engineering marvel. If any one of these thirty proteins is inactivated by genetic mutation, the whole apparatus will fail to work properly.[29]

Indeed, it looks as if this structure has such irreducible complexity that it requires a special design step. Could any of these components have evolved by chance unless the other twenty-nine had developed at the same time? It seems evident that none of these parts could have evolved by mutation and natural selection until the entire structure had been assembled. And other examples of complexity seem to defy similar claims made by evolutionary theory. Just think of the human blood-clotting cascade, with its dozen or more interacting proteins, or the complexity of the human eye. Natural selection can't work until the entire structure has been assembled.

Indeed, it looks as if evolutionary theory has taken a hit from falsification. And ID fans are eager to jump into the gap allegedly left behind by introducing an alternative (or at least additional) mechanism for evolution, based on the notion of intelligent design interventions. But let's not jump to conclusions, for ID faces some serious problems.

## 1. Science and the argument from design

A first objection concerns the use of Paley's argument from design in science. Prior to any talk of evolutionary theory, William Paley had argued that something as beautifully designed as the universe must have had a Designer, just like a watch does. I think it's important to acknowledge that the argument has basically two versions. To explain this, I'd like to introduce here the difference between a necessary and a sufficient condition. Having a battery in your car is a necessary condition for your car to start. Without a battery, your car will not start. But would it also be a sufficient condition? Of course not, for having a battery in the car does not guarantee that your car will start; there are many other conditions needed for that to happen. Or consider this example: Having oxygen in the earth's atmosphere is a necessary condition in life. However, having oxygen will not guarantee human life; there are many other conditions needed for human life other than oxygen in the atmosphere. A sufficient condition brings

---

29. Francis Collins, *The Language of God* (New York: Free Press, 2006), 185.

about an effect, but doesn't rule out that the same effect could come from other causes. So with this in mind, let's look at the two versions of this argument about design.

&#10022; If there is design, there is a Designer, God (and then the argument continues: Well, there is design, so there *must* be a Designer—which makes God a logically *necessary* condition: no Designer, then no design). In other words, having a Designer is a necessary condition in order to have design (but doesn't necessarily guarantee design, because the Designer could choose not to make anything).

&#10022; If there is a Designer, God, there is design (and then the argument continues: Well, there is a Designer, so there *must* be design— which makes God a logically *sufficient* condition: no design, then no Designer). In other words, having a Designer guarantees that there will be design. But this doesn't rule out that design could come about from other causes—such as natural selection.

ID theorists use the first version and claim they have found a scientifically conclusive argument for introducing a Designer into the theory of evolution: A watch is complex and has a designer; life is complex and therefore, by analogy, must also have a Designer. However, within a purely *scientific* context, this version doesn't perform well; complexity and design are not logically sufficient reasons for, or logical proof of, the existence of a Designer. The fact that two entities share the characteristic of complexity doesn't logically imply they must share all other characteristics as well. Man and ape are both mammals, for example, but that doesn't mean they both have fur. Correspondingly, the fact that a watch and an organism are both complex doesn't imply by logical necessity, let alone scientific evidence, that they both must have an intelligent designer as well. Analogy is just not compelling enough to make us believe in God. Would the intricate structure and order of snowflakes and diamonds really require any Designer's intervention?

The way ID proponents like to interpret the argument from design would be a sneaky way of smuggling God back into the scientific arena, making him a stowaway or captive of science. However, science can't accept this argument; as I said earlier, it must *assume* design but can't *explain* it. The argument from design is not a logical or scientific argument that conclusively forces us to reason from design toward a Designer. This is perhaps the point that John Henry Cardinal Newman (1801–1890; a convert recently declared Blessed) was making when he said about Paley's argument from design that seeing design doesn't make him (Newman) believe in God.[30] Saint Thomas Aquinas would probably have said that the Creator or Designer is a Primary Cause, not a secondary cause in the way a watchmaker is a secondary cause. The existence and the impact of a Creator Designer can never be proven the way we prove things in logic or science. Among natural explanations, there is no place for supernatural explanations. It is this version of the argument from design that Darwin considers defeated by his theory of natural selection: "The old argument of design in nature, as given by Paley, which formerly seemed to me so conclusive, fails, now that the law of natural selection has been discovered."[31] *Biological* designs have indeed been tested by the filter of natural selection.

It would be much better and safer to interpret the argument from design as stating the opposite: "If there is a Designer, there is design"— and not the other way around. This second interpretation is more like an "argument *to* design" than an "argument *from* design." Saint Thomas Aquinas comes much closer to this version of the argument than the other version when he discusses his so-called *Five Ways*—all of which are essentially just one way, the *Third Way* from contingency: Nothing on earth explains itself as to why it is as it is, or why it exists at all. In fact, these "ways" are not presented as logical arguments or conclusive proofs of God's existence in a *logical* sense, but when taken in a *rational* sense, they offer strong reasons (arguments) for his existence, which makes them work like powerful pointers to a Creator God as the best possible (and probably only) *rational* explanation for the way this universe is. The Five Ways are not so much logical or *scientific* proofs of God's existence as they are *philosophical* clarifications of what we mean when we speak of God and what the consequences are of the way we understand God. We either accept that nothing explains itself and leave it at that—which is basically irrational—or we restore rationality by stating that nothing explains itself *and therefore needs a Creator God.* All of this is a powerful answer to the question: How could there be order and design in this universe if there were no Designer? How else could we rationally explain

---

30. In a letter of April 13, 1870, to Mr. Brownlow.

31. *Autobiography*, 59, 87.

the existence of order and design? The existence of a Creator God is the best *rational* explanation of this universe; it takes the way this world happens to be as a particular cosmic design that the Designer *chose* from among all possible designs.

Saint Thomas had no intention of logically proving God's existence. Why would he want to logically prove that God exists anyway? Believers don't need to prove it (and atheists don't want to); besides, there were no declared atheists at his time. Instead, the Five Ways clarify what it entails when we speak of God, and they show that belief in God is actually the most *rational* step to take. That's why Saint Thomas does not conclude his reasoning with, "Therefore, God exists," but by the less overreaching statement, "And this all men think of as God." But again, that's the domain of philosophy and religion, not of science. In science, design is a given, a presupposition; but in philosophy, design would be explained by deriving it from something or rather Someone Else (in an argument *to* design). Unlike the other version, this version of the argument certainly remains untouched by Darwin's theory of natural selection, for his theory must assume some kind of *cosmic* design in order for natural selection to be able to filter biological designs. Where this cosmic design comes from is a question beyond the reach of science.

So God may not be at the *end* of a logical argument (as an inevitable conclusion), but rather at its *beginning*; a divine Designer is the *origin* of all design and thus a logically sufficient reason or rational explanation for design—otherwise the concept of design would be an irrational assumption. Whereas science must *assume* design, philosophy and religion can *explain* it by deriving it from a Creator God. I think Blessed Cardinal Newman was probably right when he said that he believes in design because he believes in God (and not the other way around).[32] Seen in the light of creation, we know the universe is God's design, because we know there is a God, a Creator and Designer—otherwise we would have no rational explanation as to why the universe is the way it is.

The claim of ID theorists that *science* can discern a Designer is therefore off the mark. *Philosophy*, however, may be able to achieve this (as I keep trying to bring across), but science itself has definitely no direct access to God or a Designer. There is a dividing fence between science and

---

32. In a letter of April 13, 1870, to Mr. Brownlow.

philosophy/religion, but ID fans just don't like to be confined to one side of the fence; they prefer sitting on the fence itself in order to jump back and forth—which makes for improper why-answers to how-questions, and improper how-answers to why-questions. It's precisely for that reason that there must be proper boundaries between science and religion, so we can renounce pseudoscience and semireligion.

ID, however, is right in one respect: Science does assume some form of preexisting, intelligent design of the universe, a cosmic design structure of order, including causality and functionality (teleology). And this very fact of order and functionality makes biological designs functioning and *intelligible*, but not necessarily *intelligent*. The fact that all biological designs follow the rules of the *cosmic* design (in the *meta*physical sense) explains why specific *biological* designs do function and achieve their goal. But the fact *that* they work successfully and effectively (a creation issue) is altogether different from the question as to *how* specific cases of biological design came along (an evolution issue). Whether biological designs are successful or not is determined by the cosmic design of *creation*, but how those came along is a matter of *evolution*.

In short, biological designs are like pilot balloons, created tentatively to be tested against the cosmic design during the process of natural selection. If there is any intelligence in creation, it resides in the realm of *cosmic* design, but not directly or necessarily in the realm of *biological* designs. Biological designs presuppose a metaphysical design, and this metaphysical design is best understood as an intelligent cosmic design of creation. The cosmic design is an *intelligent* design, since it is the creation of an Intelligent Designer, but biological designs are evolutionary products successful to different degrees, with some designs being better than others—or appearing more intelligently designed than others, if you will. If biological designs seem intelligently designed, they are so in a *derivative* sense.

So we shouldn't try to change natural selection into supernatural selection. Because supernatural actions do not square well with the natural sciences, we do not have to invoke them when natural causes will do. All processes in nature follow physical and biological laws. These laws control everything in the universe, including the evolution of life (of course, it is God who gave these laws domain over the entire universe). If a Big Bang actually happened, the physical laws and boundary conditions must have existed before the Big Bang, providing a framework in which even the Big

Bang had to take place. These laws are part of the intelligent cosmic design of creation and have their origin in an intelligent, lawgiving Creator. But we shouldn't bring God back in again to steer, adjust, or redirect his own laws. God doesn't need to keep the planets moving, nor does he need to keep species evolving; they just follow their God-given laws. But again, everything would return to nothing at the very moment God were to take his breath away.

## 2. Selective use of the argument from design

Second, ID theorists are usually rather selective about when to call upon their "argument from design." They are generally eager to usher in their theory when biological features become so "complex" that additional divine intervention seems necessary. At that point, ID fans like to point out that natural selection won't work until the entire structure has been assembled, because some structures presumably cannot function until all their substructures are present. To explain such complex structures, we are supposed to invoke an intelligent cause operational within the process of evolution—that is, some form of immediate divine intervention. If these ID theorists were right, evolution would require constant supernatural mediation.

I would like to offer two objections to this idea of the ID theorists. First, the notion of design is *always* needed as a philosophical presupposition, even for the most basic cases of functionality, no matter whether it is a plain form of passive camouflage like green caterpillars or a much more intricate kind such as the active coloration of an octopus. So the degree of complexity doesn't really matter. Second, we should stress that complexity is an ambiguous issue. I admit that information theory allows us to quantify complexity and specification, but so what? Besides, complexity often emerges from a high degree of interactivity. So, how complex do features have to be to get beyond the reach of natural processes? If *losing* wing functionality (e.g., in penguins) is a common evolutionary process, why wouldn't *developing* wing functionality be one too? ID fans would counter that this latter functionality has to be designed first—in full and all at once. Are they right?

Let's take the example of the human heart, a sophisticated organ. We share this type of heart with all other mammals. If one single part of this complex structure fails, the entire structure may be in trouble. Could this complexity have evolved step by step, little by little? I don't see why not. Actually, we do find indications of a gradual evolutionary process—starting with one atrium and one ventricle (in fish), then a double atrium (in amphibians), next an almost fully split ventricle (in reptiles), and finally, in mammals, a double atrium and a double ventricle so that low-oxygen blood remains fully separated from high-oxygen blood—which makes indeed for a fancy high-pressure cardiovascular design. Was this process beyond the reach of mutation and natural selection? I don't see why it would have to be.

Yet in such a case, ID theorists would invoke the intervention of an Intelligent Designer, as they tend to call upon *intelligent design* for relatively complex examples of biological design anytime they think evolutionary theory alone cannot explain it. However, if *intelligent design* is indeed a *meta*physical precondition of evolution, then it is a precondition of any evolutionary development, no matter whether the outcome is complex or more simple. I consider even the relatively simple structure of proteins as quite complex; the world of amino acids shows a very intricate design.

## 3. The problem of flawed designs

Third, biology offers many concrete cases of design in nature that are far from flawless—designs that just don't look very intelligent. How is this compatible with an intervening, truly intelligent Designer who supposedly crafted all examples of design by divine, supernatural, and miraculous intervention, on a case-by-case basis? I admit it is hard to tell what qualifies as an ideal and intelligent design, and what does not. Besides, the ID theorist can always escape by claiming that God decided to do things the imperfect way. But the point here is that evolutionary theory does not have this problem of imperfect designs because natural selection goes for optimal designs (the best of what's available), not perfect designs—let alone intelligent designs.

Take the case of the panda's thumb. Although they belong to the order Carnivora, all of which lack an opposable thumb, giant pandas came to subsist on a diet of bamboo, which requires a means to grasp shoots. So a bone in the wrist has become extended to serve as part of a grasping device—thus creating a rudimentary thumb in addition to five fingers. The outcome is odd, clumsy, and inefficient, probably a disgrace to a competent Designer. But natural selection can explain why it happened this way. The quality of evolutionary designs can be as diverse as the quality of machine designs. Natural selection goes for the best design among the presently available biological designs. Isn't that a reasonable explanation for the panda's thumb? With respect to unforeseen future needs, the original design indeed seems shortsighted.

We know of many examples of optimal designs (the best of what's available) that are not perfect designs, let alone intelligent designs. Yet, ID proponents prefer to disregard these examples. Instead, they offer us the miraculous scenario of a supernatural intelligent intervention in cases of their choosing. But would this really make the scars of past evolutionary steps disappear? I seriously doubt that. My response would be that we have here that infamous Divine Foot in the door again. Invoking divine interventions means that God has to regularly fix the inadequacies of his own initial designs. Thus we have made God the executor of our own wills! I am attacking here not God, but ID theorists.

Of course, it is not God who needs to fix inadequacies in his designs, but it is this imaginary, fabricated "designer" who was eagerly concocted by the ID theory to occasionally interfere in the process of evolution—at times that the ID theory deems intervention necessary. I think that we should not go that route. If there is intelligence in creation—and I strongly believe there is—then it resides in the realm of *cosmic* design, but not necessarily in the realm of specific *biological* designs. The cosmic design is an intelligent design, since it is the creation of an Intelligent Designer, but individual biological designs are successful to different degrees. Some designs are better than others—or some seem more "intelligently designed" than others, if you will.

## 4. The problem of rudimentary designs

This leads to a fourth objection. Many "designs" in nature look not just clumsy but indeed rudimentary, underdeveloped, undersized, stunted, or broken—again, not very "intelligent." I mentioned earlier the DNA sequence for an enzyme that makes for ascorbic acid (vitamin C) in most animals. Vitamin C is a potent antioxidant and is a cofactor in several vital enzymatic reactions. Many primates, including humans, have a defect in this DNA code—so it became a pseudogene. Consequently, these organisms must acquire vitamin C through food (which was abundant for our arboreal ancestors anyway), but they did hold on to its repetitive sequences in the "silent" section of their DNA.

So what we have here is a "broken" design plus nonworking repetitions of the original design. That doesn't look like a very efficient or intelligent design, no matter how we define those adjectives. Why would a Designer first design the vitamin C pathway and then destroy it? I have never found a sensible, let alone intelligent, ID answer. But some ID theorists tried to avoid this difficulty by stating that DNA duplicates are actually a new intelligent invention—a Designer's backup strategy, so to speak. It's hard to hit a target that keeps moving. ID theorists owe us some more adequate answers.

In general, cases of rudimentary designs are hard to reconcile with "intelligent design" as an operational intervening factor with foresight. The theory of natural selection, on the other hand, can explain these cases as "leftovers" from common descent with modification. Of course, ID backers could always fall back on the position that the Intelligent Designer may have planned everything to make it *look* as if it was the outcome of an evolutionary process! But that brings us back to an unbeatable conspiracy theory that adapts like a chameleon to all kinds of circumstances and explains nothing by explaining everything. In science, such patchwork is forbidden.

Another example of an obsolete design is the gene for a jaw muscle protein (MYH16), which has become a pseudogene in humans but still functions to develop strong jaw muscles in other primates. The list could go on and on: the existence of useless wings in flightless birds such as ostriches and penguins, or the potentially fatal condition of appendicitis, which is caused by an appendix that has lost its function, but is or was highly developed in herbivores, aiding in the bacterial digestion of cellulose. According to evolutionary theory, all these instances of rudimentary designs are scars or leftovers of original designs inherited from ancestors. What would ID do with such cases, other than ignore them? Or even worse: If these design "flaws" were really the deliberate products of an intelligent Designer's intervention, then the Designer must be either inept or sadistic. ID theorists love to impress us with examples of complex designs, while turning a blind eye to cases of rudimentary, stunted, or even broken designs. Isn't this a highly selective perception? Of course, the one to blame in these failed design cases is not God, but the "designer" who was concocted by the ID theory in order to occasionally and miraculously fix evolutionary problems—at any moment that the ID theory deems intervention necessary and then summons a Designer. ID theorists have not offered convincing responses to these objections.

## 5. Cosmic design as a necessary framework

The fifth objection is similar to one made earlier against creationism. Some ID theorists mix up causes and functions on the one side, and origins, purposes, and destinations on the other side, throwing them all in the same bag. While science works with causal and functional accounts in natural terms, it does not and cannot allow for supernatural explanations based on a design maker. Yet, as I have often stressed, science must—and does—accept the concept of design as a philosophical presupposition, for the simple reason that the cosmic design concept provides the necessary framework in which natural selection can and must operate. If that's the case, intelligent design does not work at the level of *evolution*, but belongs to the paramount, overarching, surpassing, and transcending level of *creation*. ID theorists tend to confuse these two levels or ignore their distinction. Design, in science, is a *meta*physical *assumption*, and therefore cannot be a physical *cause* at the same time. All we need in evolution is the cosmic design of *creation* to channel the biological designs of *evolution*—but Designer interventions are out of the question. God is the *source* of all being, not a superbeing among other beings who acts like other beings.

At the very moment, however, that we would allow a Designer to become a scientific concept, we bring in God as a physical, or at least intervening, causal link to explain the gaps in our current scientific knowledge. By so doing, we run the risk, sooner or later, of pushing God and his designing interventions back whenever science makes progress. As a matter of policy, it is imprudent to build one's case for faith on what science has not yet explained, because tomorrow science may be able to explain it. Never give in to the temptation of finding God in what we still don't know, for then we are apt to be discredited by the latest news of success on the scientific front. So let's not invoke "miracles" where they don't belong. God is not a response to a need.

Yet, even Isaac Newton fell for this timeless temptation of having God keep a Divine Foot in the door, when he called upon God's active intervention to periodically re-form the solar system from increasing irregularities, to prevent the stars from falling in on one another, and perhaps even to keep the amount of motion in the universe from decaying due to viscosity and friction. Today, we know God doesn't have to make these interventions, because science can now explain them with the proper laws (which are God's laws anyway).

We should learn from Johannes Kepler, who changed the circular orbits of Copernicus' heliocentric model into elliptical orbits because he knew God would not tolerate the inaccuracy that plagued the older models. History teaches us again and again that a God of the Gaps often proves to be a fleeting illusion; it is a god in disguise. And this point takes me to the next objection.

## 6. Complexity and gradual development

The sixth and main problem with ID is that as a matter of fact, science seems to have reached a stage where "irreducible" complexity can actually be reduced to step-by-step evolutionary processes of mutations and natural selection (without the need of invoking an additional Designer step). Let us go back to the bacterial flagellum, the favorite example of ID fans. Comparing protein sequences from various bacteria reveals that several components of the flagellum are related to an entirely different apparatus used by some bacteria to inject toxins into other bacteria—which in itself is an ideal target for natural selection. Most likely, the elements of this structure were duplicated in DNA and then recruited for a new use, subject to natural selection. And in turn, this process could go on for other elements. Selection just keeps working step by step (mutation by mutation, gene by gene) until the entire structure has been assembled.

Think of the following analogy: Once the keystone is placed in an arched stone bridge, the scaffolding can be removed; from then on, removing any part may cause the bridge to collapse, yet the bridge is still the product of a gradual construction process. So what is left of the "irreducible complexity" of a system wherein, according to ID proponents, removing any of its parts is supposed to cause the system to effectively cease functioning? Less and less evidence can be found to support that idea.

We may assume a similar scenario of step-by-step selection for the intricate cascading route of human blood clotting, involving many proteins (also called "factors"; most hemophiliacs carry a mutated version of factor VIII, some of factor IX). Most of these proteins are related to one another at the level of amino acid sequence, which most likely reflects ancient gene duplications. Since new copies were not essential for the original function, they could gradually evolve to take on a new function, driven by the force of mutation and natural selection. So the ID assumption seems superfluous: namely, that the entire cascade (or units of it) had to emerge fully functional from the very outset as a complete set of DNA sequences. If ID theorists object: "What good is half an eye?" I would reply "Better than no eye at all." This can be exemplified by the partial clotting cascades found in fish: Isn't a partial cascade far better than none? As a matter of fact, the blood clotting mechanism did evolve from a low-pressure to a high-pressure cardio-vascular system when needed to stop possible leaks quickly. So there goes the divine intervention of a Designer as a causal and intelligent factor in biological explanations! Another gap has been closed, despite the claims of ID fans.

Even if evolutionary theory still cannot explain some cases of irreducible complexity, those cases do not prove ID. If one theory cannot explain certain parts of evolution yet, that doesn't make the competing theory true. Let us not forget that the unexplained is not necessarily unexplainable, the unknown unknowable, or the unsolved unsolvable. Only time will tell. Avery Cardinal Dulles, SJ, wisely remarked, "If the production of organs [sic] such as the *bacterial flagellum* can be explained by the gradual accumulation of minor random variations, the Darwinist explanation should be preferred"[33] (over the ID theory, that is). Cardinal Dulles was basically telling us not to invoke supernatural causes in science when natural causes will do (and should do, I would add).

## 7. Faith and reason

The seventh objection to ID theory is that it defies the motto that runs like a thread through the history of the Catholic Church (and therefore, through this book)—namely, "faith and reason." This may strike you as an

---

33. Avery Dulles, SJ, "God and Evolution," *First Things*, October 2007: 19–24.

unexpected counterargument, but ID theory has actually abandoned both faith and reason.

To begin with, ID theory does injustice to *faith*, for faith takes the universe as a *whole* that is created by God our Creator. ID theory, however, turns this perfect whole into a *defective* whole that is not causally complete in itself, but requires additional causes to fill the voids God supposedly left behind. ID fans tout intelligent design as a scientific concept, although it is a metaphysical presupposition, not a physical, causal explanation. However, once taken as a *meta*physical *assumption*, intelligent design cannot be a physical *cause* at the same time; it can no longer be used to fill in the gaps left behind in the allegedly defective design of the universe.

In addition, ID theory does injustice to *reason* and rationality because it anticipates that science cannot do its job without taking refuge in unscientific principles. The history of science shows us various examples:

❖ In the seventeenth century, chemistry had its so-called *phlogiston* theory. Phlogiston was supposed to be a substance that is liberated during burning, but it had no color, odor, taste, or mass—and was therefore immeasurable and unscientific.

❖ The theory of *spontaneous generation* dates back to Aristotle, but was popular until the twentieth century. It states that living organisms can spontaneously arise or develop from nonliving matter through some kind of mystifying "life force"; in other words, living material can die, but "vital forces" cannot.

❖ For a while, chemistry also held the theory that fermentation (with enzymes) would only be possible due to an immaterial life force residing in a living cell.

❖ Around 1900, embryology entertained the theory of *entelechy*, which postulated that some mysterious goal-oriented and organizing principle directs the development of embryos, until biologists realized that DNA and other material factors provided a more rational explanation.

In all these cases, the theory at issue was not overthrown by experiments—it didn't meet the criteria for experiments. Such a theory turns out to be an unscientific principle that is perhaps still useful and valid outside the scientific realm. Louis Pasteur, for instance, did not experimentally defeat the doctrine that life can arise spontaneously, but he decided to define all air giving rise to life as contaminated with germs, thus creating a concept that can be measured and controlled. In other words, what is at stake here is not a *false* theory but an *unscientific* theory, unbeatable by nature. But I admit that in order to identify such theories as unscientific a good scientific alternative is often needed, helping us to differentiate more clearly between scientific and unscientific theories. Debates like these actually made scientists more aware of what it means for science to be *empirical*.

I would say that ID theory is the next theory in line to end up on the unscientific side of the divide. It claims that biological complexity as a natural phenomenon is inherently beyond natural explanation, and therefore calls for an immaterial, supernatural principle. Isn't that the breakdown of reason? In essence, ID theory claims that, in terms of regular science, the unknown is ultimately unknowable and the unsolved unsolvable; ID fans have given up on science ahead of time. Scientists, on the other hand, expect that all natural phenomena are explainable, since it is their basic belief that nature displays order and intelligibility, making it possible for the human mind to investigate it. Science that oversteps its limits is arrogant, but science that does not go to its limits is a failure.

Saint Albert advises us "to turn to a theologian in matters of faith, but to a physician or scientist in matters of medicine or physics."[34] So let's turn to a biologist in matters of evolution, and not to an ID theorist. And Saint Albert writes decisively that "Natural science does not consist in ratifying what others have said, but in seeking the causes of phenomena." Let us seek those causes! Evolution follows God's laws as much as DNA does.

As Charles Darwin wrote in a letter, "astronomers do not state that God directs the course of each comet and planet."[35] He was right: comets and planets simply follow laws. Why wouldn't the same hold for the process of evolution? If losing wing functionality (e.g., in penguins) is a regular evolutionary process, why wouldn't developing wing functionality be one, too? Therefore, science has the task and obligation to find the laws that regulate the processes taking place in our universe, without invoking miracle steps where they don't belong. Science has no place for miracles—they

---

34. Elsewhere, Saint Albert says, "The aim of natural science is not simply to accept the statements of others, but to investigate the causes that are at work in nature" (*De Mineralium et Rebus Metallicis*, lib. II, tr. ii, i).

35. In correspondence with geologist Charles Lyell in 1861.

go against science's aim of detecting causes and laws that allow us to explain and predict. Invoking miracles in science is like making a move in chess after you have been checkmated; you are not making any move at all, because you are no longer playing chess. Invoking miracles in science is like soccer players trying to score a goal on their own side. The Catholic convert and novelist Graham Greene couldn't have worded it better regarding the miracle of a man raised from the dead: ". . . they say: there aren't miracles, it is simply that we have enlarged our conception of what life is. Now we know you can be alive without pulse, breath, heartbeats. And they invent a new word to describe that state of life."[36] Indeed, that's what science would do; miracles are not to be found within the scientific realm, but they do belong to the realm of religion.

Nevertheless, ID theory keeps God busy with miraculously interrupting his own laws in order to adjust and redirect their outcome. This violates the rule of faith and reason. God should never become a miraculous step in scientific reasoning. It is, again, as if God and the Colorado River were competing candidates for carving out the Grand Canyon. So please do not summon God (or a divine Designer) when science is not yet able to do the job. Science and religion belong to different domains that operate under different rules. We need to respect those rules while recognizing that "Science and technology by their very nature require unconditional respect for fundamental moral criteria."[37]

Let's come to a conclusion. ID proponents not only wage a battle against evolutionism and its devoted believers—a cause I applaud—but they also maintain they've found a theory that competes with evolutionary theory itself—a claim I question and dispute. ID theorists try to introduce *meta*physical (perhaps even religious) concepts into the arena of science, where physical causes and biological functions should reign and operate. Intelligent Design may be a legitimate metaphysical notion, but only outside the domain of science. As such, it is not an intrascientific but an extrascientific concept that would be considered foreign in science since it originated in the *meta*physical realm. We can't introduce metaphysical notions into science. Be aware, natural selection must *assume* design but can neither explain nor create it.

---

36. Graham Greene, *The Power and the Glory* (New York, Viking Press, 1970), 270.
37. *CCC*, no. 2294.

ID theory is not a worldview or ideology the way evolutionism and creationism are, and at least it doesn't read the Book of Nature in terms of the Book of Scripture. But beyond that it appears to be, to use chemical terminology, an amalgam of disparate, incompatible elements. Using a biological metaphor, I would consider it a hybrid that has lost its fertility. In more general terms, I would label it an impossible dream.

Why do I still call *Intelligent Design* a dream then? It certainly would be a beautiful dream if it were true because we do need divine help—no matter whether such help comes from philosophy or religion. But at the same time, this dream, beautiful as it may be, is an *impossible* dream the way ID theorists take it, because in science there is no space for divine design-designers, or for any other unscientific concepts or supernatural steps. It is a dream beyond the reach of science. Science cannot accept unscientific principles such as phlogiston, vital force, or entelechy—or intelligent design, for that matter. We can't infiltrate science with unscientific theories, for good fences make good neighbors (of course, on condition that both sides respect those fences). We shouldn't even poke our fingers through the fence, for they could be bitten off. In science, we cannot invoke unscientific principles.

Consequently, we must state that God and *Intelligent Design* are beyond the reach of science. And yet, we seem to desperately need a divine Designer. That's why I keep calling it a *beautiful* dream, because we do need help from "outside," given that there is more to life than science. I would love for this dream to come true—but not the way the ID theory suggests. Is there any other way? Thank God, there is . . .

## Summary of Objections Against . . .

| Evolutionism | Creationism | Intelligent Design Theory |
| --- | --- | --- |
| Monopolistic worldview | Two incompatible reports in Genesis | Flawed argument from design |
| Self-defeating enterprise | Intellectual suicide | Design is not only for complexity |
| Restricted outlook on life | Problem of flawed designs | Problems of clumsy designs |
| No blind agent called fate | A mix-up of hows and whys | Problem of obsolete designs |
| No order out of disorder | Creation has no chronology | A mixup of hows and whys |
| Baseless worldview | God is no innerworldly cause | Complexity may be reducible |
| Dangerous implications | Monopolistic worldview | A breakdown of reason |

=========== DELVING DEEPER ===========

Evolution by Chance? What Does That Mean?

What do biologists mean when they say that something happens at random or by chance?

Mutations in genetic material are considered to happen by chance. What do scientists mean when they say this? First, they mean that mutations are *unpredictable* (as far as we know) as to when and where they strike. Second, mutations are *unrelated*, since there is no connection with anything else going on (other than radiation or chemical pollutants). Third, mutations are also *arbitrary*, because mutations do not select their target but hit indiscriminately. Fourth, mutations are *opportunistic*, because they occur regardless of any future needs. But as soon as we get to the last meaning of chance in the chart—being meaningless and without a purpose—we have left the territory of science. Some people would like to go that far, though, by taking chance to be another name for a capricious, blind agent called fate. I would say this outlook is chance with a capital C—the goddess of Fate. Science has nothing to say about chance with a capital C. Fate is far beyond its reach; fate is in essence a worldview.

Environmental changes are also considered to happen "by chance." Those changes may be *predictable* (based on things like climatology), but they do happen "by chance" in being *arbitrary* (without any preference for a certain location). They are also *undirected* because they don't strive for a preset goal. Of course, there is no chance with a capital C here; doom, blind fate, and random destiny are definitely out of the picture.

Chance also plays a role in genetics. When male organisms produce sperm cells or when female organisms produce ova, it is a matter of chance which chromosome parts get exchanged (recombination through crossovers) and which single gene (allele) of each pair of genes ends up in each reproductive cell. In these cases, chance is mostly a matter of "no preference" and "no foresight." Yet, some predictability is involved (for example, according to Mendel's statistical laws) as well as some correlation (such as that genes may be linked). Never, however, is the outcome of the next generation orchestrated by the goddess of Fate; no one is genetically doomed or favored by blind destiny.

What about natural selection? It only happens by chance in one particular sense: it makes a population adapt to a volatile environment, regardless of what the future has to bring. This may turn out to be an opportunistic, short-sighted adaptation (microevolution), but in and of itself it is highly selective. It is definitely not random in the sense of arbitrary. But it seems true that microevolution does not have a direction other than instant adaptation. For example, if air pollution gives dark peppered moths that rest on soot-blackened trees an effective camouflage (so that more of them appear in the next generations), a reversal of the pollution would favor the lighter variants again. Obviously, selection can go either way; if you would film the first part, playing the film backward wouldn't seem strange. Sometimes, organs first develop and then degenerate. But no matter how selection operates, chance with a capital C is absolutely out of the question.

Evolution on a larger scale (macroevolution), however, is a more ambiguous issue in science. If macroevolution is only lingering microevolution, it would also be an undirected, shortsighted phenomenon. Nevertheless, some biologists prefer to see a long-term trend in evolution toward more complexity, more efficiency, more independence, and more intelligence (in spite of seeming oscillations). Were we to play such an evolutionary movie backward, we would say it is going the wrong way, something like a stream running uphill—which means that somehow we do perceive some kind of direction in evolution. The time arrow in evolution seems to move from less complex to more complex, whatever that means. Again, no matter which side we take in this scientific debate, the idea of chance with a capital C is again completely outside our scientific scope.

I will make one more remark about macroevolution. The built-in order of the universe could very well steer microevolution in the direction of more complexity. The evolutionary pathway followed so far was to a certain extent preordained by the intrinsic properties of the materials involved, given a certain kind of environment or succession of environmental conditions. Because of those intrinsic properties and constraints of a *created* universe—that is, due to the cosmic design of creation—we might go as far as to speculate that our world was bound, by its very nature, to give birth to life, perhaps even to human life. Arguably, nature has been endowed with the capacity of developing life and human life, and as such it would surely be an "intelligent project." What we see operating during evolution is an order from within, a cosmic order, that did not develop itself but was there from the beginning, making biological designs work. But that's where science has reached its boundaries, since we enter here the arena of philosophy and religion.

Some people have questioned what the "selecting agent" is behind natural selection. Did Darwin replace God with the goddess of nature? It may seem so, but I would say instead that it is the cosmic design of creation that determines which biological designs are effective and successful. An analogy can take this idea a bit farther. A river follows its path according to the topographic design of the landscape. In a similar way, the stream of evolution follows a path regulated by the cosmic design behind our universe, so it follows a path of least resistance. French molecular biologist and Nobel laureate Jacques Monod titled one of his books *Le Hasard et la Nécessité*. Although I don't agree with the way he interprets this pairing, I will adapt it to my terminology and use it for the distinction between scientific randomness and philosophical necessity—that is, between the scientific randomness of a randomly meandering evolutionary stream and the philosophical necessity imposed by the cosmic design of the evolutionary landscape. To put it differently, the stream of evolution actually runs in the bed of cosmic design.

## Does Pope Benedict XVI Favor Intelligent Design?

Recently, some have speculated that that Pope Benedict XVI is almost ready to endorse ID theory. Is this really going to happen? Of course, I don't have the foresight (or the connections) to know what Pope Benedict is going to do, but I can at least make an educated guess.

First, the Holy Father is not referring to the *theory* of Intelligent Design, which pretends to be a scientific theory, additional to or as an alternative for the theory of natural selection. Instead, Pope Benedict prefers to speak in terms of an "intelligent project" or plan—which I have been referring to as the intelligence of the cosmic design. He said once that atheists have worked hard to make many believe that "it is scientific to think that all things lack guidance and order as though they were at the mercy of chance." In response, he says, "In the beginning [is] the creative Word—this Word that created all things, that created this intelligent design which is the cosmos."[38] That's where the Pope makes room for explanations beyond scientific limits.

The Pope is not criticizing evolutionary theory itself but rather *evolutionism*, which does indeed deny any direction or order in evolution and does not allow for explanations beyond scientific limits. It is right here that the philosophical and religious notion of creation and design comes into play to fill the void that science necessarily leaves behind, as I have stressed throughout this entire book. Obviously, the Pope is favoring the philosophical notion of an "intelligent project," not to be confused with the presumably scientific *theory* of "intelligent design." Intelligent design is an essential element of *creation*, but not an interfering factor in *evolution*; it is the intelligence of the *cosmic* design behind all *biological* designs.

Pope Benedict XVI continues a long Catholic tradition of honoring faith and reason, religion and science. Therefore, it is hard to believe that he wouldn't take scientific developments seriously. Yet he should and always will fight any ideologies such as evolutionism that claim to be based on science only, yet violate reason. I have strong reasons to consider Pope Benedict a relentless defender of faith and reason, in spite of some media reports to the contrary.

A reason for some of these rumors is that Christoph Cardinal Schönborn, OP, a friend of Pope Benedict and the general editor of the *Catechism of the Catholic Church*, explicitly mentioned the words "intelligent design" on several occasions. He explained, from his episcopal residence in central Vienna,[39] that he wanted to make clear where the Church thinks scientists overstep their bounds. "The Church's task now is to defend reason," he said, citing as his inspiration his former theology professor Joseph Ratzinger, now Pope Benedict. "The theory of evolution is a *scientific* theory," the cardinal said. "What I call evolutionism is an *ideological* view that says evolution can explain everything in the whole development of the cosmos, from the Big Bang to Beethoven's Ninth Symphony" (emphasis added). I couldn't agree more.

Cardinal Schönborn has spelled out a position that respects Darwin's achievements but rejects neo-Darwinian views that go beyond what science can prove. He said he agrees with ID theory that the complexity of

---

38. General audience, November 9, 2005.

39. In an interview with Reuters, November 2005.

life clearly points to a superior intelligence that must have devised this system—as an "intelligent project" or "intelligible plan," I might add. True, he did mention the *theory* of ID, but he based this insight solely on reason—"neither on theology nor modern science nor 'intelligent design theory,'" as he clarified later.[40] Then the cardinal added, "The next step is to ask—which intelligence? As a believer, of course, I think it is the intelligence of the Creator." I would say again I couldn't agree more, but I also repeat that this is not in any way an endorsement for the *theory* of ID. This intelligence cannot come from science, but is to be found through philosophy—as important a tool of reason as science. Intelligent design is not an interfering factor in *evolution*, but it certainly is an essential part of *creation*. I could also say it differently: Nothing in evolution makes sense except in the light of creation.

Let me take this thought one step farther. Due to the framework of intelligent design in which the intelligent project of evolution operates, we as human beings have been able to emerge as intelligent designers ourselves, capable of designing structures guided by art, architecture, engineering, and scientific research. That's why the *Catechism* can state that scientific "discoveries invite us to even greater admiration for the greatness of the Creator, prompting us to give him thanks for all his works and for the understanding and wisdom he gives to scholars and researchers."[41] All this leads us to the religious conviction that God has created the world according to an intelligible plan that is accessible to the human intellect through the natural light of reason.

Unfortunately, the distinctions made here are intricate and may seem rather highbrow. That may explain why the discussion often gets muddled in the media. There is no indication that Pope Benedict XVI has joined the camp of ID proponents, although he may very well share parts of their concerns. This doesn't mean in any way, though, that Pope Benedict is likely to replace natural selection with some kind of supernatural selection. In line with Pope John Paul II, he fully respects the fences between good neighbors. But he is absolutely right that those fences must be respected by *both* camps. Saint Gregory, bishop of Nyssa (c. 335–c. 395), one of the Cappadocian Fathers and a theologian much respected by Pope Benedict,

---

40. In *First Things*, January 2006.
41. *CCC*, no. 283.

phrased it this way: "The mystery of theology is one thing, and the scientific investigation of nature another"; and he warns us not to confuse, in his own words, theology with physiology (or vice versa).[42] And yet, they are neighbors that cannot live without each other.

42. Joseph Cardinal Ratzinger, *Biblical Interpretation in Crisis: The 1988 Erasmus Lecture*, *First Things*, April 26, 2008, http://www.firstthings.com/onthesquare/2008/04/biblical-interpretation-in-cri.

———◇◇◇◇◇———

# CHAPTER 5

# A Fair Balance:
# Creation *and* Evolution

## 5.1 There Is More to Life Than Science

Let's go back to the question posed at the beginning of this book: "Where do we come from?" and recap our findings. When searching for (physical) *causes*, evolution has an answer for us. But if we are looking for (metaphysical) *grounds*, then creation is our answer. These two answers do not compete for a person's total and final commitment, but complement each other: Creation is a precondition for evolution, but evolution is the way creation unfolds—so we have found. In other words, nothing in evolution makes sense except in the light of creation; and nothing in the animate world makes sense without evolution.

We have here a separation of two domains that should stay clear of each other without denying each other's right to existence. They each have their own authority and specialty. We saw that Harvard evolutionary biologist Stephen Jay Gould called each one a "magisterium." In contrast to the Magisterium of the Church—which is centralized through the successors of Saint Peter, ecumenical councils, and bishops—science's authority is more diffuse, spread out over academies and societies, editorial boards of scientific journals, and peer reviewers, but it still comes close to a magisterium. And consider another parallel: Just as the history of science had its extremely gifted and ingenious key players (such as Newton, Darwin,

Mendel, Pasteur, and Einstein), so the history of Christianity had its exceptionally inspired and illuminated spokespersons as well (such as Moses,
Jeremiah, Augustine, Thomas Aquinas, and John Henry Newman).

Both domains have their specific authority, comparable to the separation of church and state. State and church should be protected from each
other's interference, yet they should acknowledge each other's indispens-
able role and authority, for the simple reason that we need them both, just
never intermingled. Something similar holds for the relationship between
religion and science—science *and* religion, not science *or* religion, not science *with* religion, let alone science *versus* religion. Religion must keep
itself open to the findings of science, and science must respect what lies
outside the boundaries surrounding its inquiries. Together they make us
whole, whereas on their own, they are incomplete and underperforming.

Thus, the voice of faith does not threaten but strengthens the voice of
science, and vice versa. Put differently, science and religion are in essence
very good neighbors that can't survive without each other. So they should
live in peaceful harmony. As a matter of fact, the person of science and the
person of faith are ultimately one and the same. Our hearts should agree
with our heads—or vice versa. What we know in science and what we
believe in religion need to live together in the same human person.

Yet, religion should be protected from intrusions by science as much as
science should be protected from intrusions by religion. Science should
stay away from religious territory as much as religion should stay clear of
scientific territory. Therefore, the Church shouldn't interfere in scientific
disputes; let scientists settle their scientific disagreements among themselves. If any missing data, inconsistencies, or controversies exist in the area
of science (e.g., in evolutionary biology), let those be freely discussed in the
scientific arena, without any religious intrusion. However, the Church can
offer science necessary moral evaluations. "Science and technology ... find
in the person and in his moral values both evidence of their purpose and
awareness of their limits."[1] Science shouldn't fear any religion that stays
within its limits. And, vice versa, the Church has nothing to fear from science, unless scientists overstep their boundaries by issuing semireligious
statements. In other words, science should never silence religion (as evolutionism does) and religion should never silence science (as creationism

---

1. *CCC*, no. 2293.

does). Evolutionism was born in the minds of arrogant scientists; creationism was born in the minds of narrow-minded fundamentalists. We have the right to hear the whole story, not just the biological part that science tells us, or the religious part that comes from faith.

Seen this way, science and creation do indeed make a good match—a match made in heaven. No real conflict can exist between science and religion, since they both come from the same source, God.[2] But not only should they live together in peace, they also actually need each other, for we don't live on bread or faith alone. Religion not only needs science in a negative sense—to purify religion from error and superstition—but also in a positive way. In order for us to fly to the moon and to develop cures for cancer, we must read the Book of Nature. Where would *faith* be if we didn't have any knowledge regarding "the structure of the world and the activity of the elements" (Wis 7:17)? Similarly, not only does science need religion in a negative way—to purify science from idolatry and false absolutes—but also in a positive way. Science depends entirely on the religious understanding, found in the Book of Scripture, that the universe is rational, that human beings are rational, and that therefore a rational universe can be comprehended by rational beings, including scientists. Where would *science* be without a rational Lawgiver? Without God, scientists have no reason to trust their scientific reasoning. Whether they admit it or not, all scientists are still living off Judeo-Christian capital.

So if there is any conflict between science and religion, it is largely a conflict between some men and women of science and some men and women of religion, rather than between science itself and religion itself. Since the "division of the estate" a few centuries ago, some "legal" battles have been going on. Creationists still deny science its part of the estate; evolutionists, in turn, want full authority over the entire estate; and ID proponents, for their part, just don't acknowledge any partition. These battles are fought by small minorities, though, but no matter how good their "lawyers" are, they don't seem to have the law on their side.

But is there anything left outside the range covered by science? Is there anything left for religion to claim as its own, from the time when science annexed the domains of causes and functions? First, Kurt Gödel had already proved in his *incompleteness theorem* (3.5.4) that no coherent

---

2. See *CCC*, no. 159.

system—not even the system of science—can be completely closed.[3] Any coherent system has certain inherent limitations, so it's essentially incomplete and needs help from outside the system. Gödel even thought that we can't give a credible account of reality itself without invoking God.[4] So science must have left some territory vacant. But because it may appear as a vacuum, it may easily go unnoticed.

Second, we must realize that, when talking about "facts," we are dealing with very peculiar entities. Many people think that, by kicking a stone, they have proved the reality of a "hard fact," but they don't realize that what comes to our senses is transformed by our minds into a mental model of the external world. Thus, reality is not only a matter of kicking and touching. In other words, facts do have a rock-solid part, beyond our control, but they also have a manmade part, dependent on human *interpretation* wrapped in some kind of conceptual framework. Even when I call an object "green," I insert much more interpretation than I might think, for in calling something green I assume that it will turn gray in twilight (a rod effect in the eye) and red when receding at high speed (the Doppler effect)—to name a few. So I claim much more than I observe.

Yes, you did read it right: There are no facts without *interpretation*. Every fact is interpreted within a specific framework or—to put it differently—is seen from a specific perspective. In other words, we don't just bump into facts; instead, we generate "facts" ourselves and then test them. In observation, one is simultaneously a passive spectator and an active creator. Since facts do not exist independently of our interpretations, there is no direct way of comparing facts with reality. Let me explain:

The problem is best expressed by Plato: "How would you search for what is unknown to you?"[5] Plato noticed a paradox: we are searching for something "unknown"—otherwise we wouldn't need to search anymore, and yet it must also be "known," otherwise we wouldn't know what to search for, or wouldn't know if we did find what we were searching for. Consequently, we need provisional hypotheses, bold ideas, that work like searchlights that may help us illuminate what was in darkness before. Observation requires interpretation.

---

3. For more on this topic, see Francesco Berto, *There's Something about Gödel: The Complete Guide to the Incompleteness Theorem* (Malden, MA: John Wiley and Sons, 2010).

4. See David Goldman, "The God of the Mathematicians," *First Things*, 2010, 205, p. 45–50.

5. In his *Meno*, 80d, although Plato discussed it in an ethical context.

In other words, observations are not like pictures taken by the "camera of our eyes," for even the pictures taken by a real camera would have to be interpreted first before they could convey any information. If scientists were mere passive observers, I'll bet cameras would qualify as the best scientists! That's where hypotheses and theories come into the picture. They are like searchlights that may bring new facts to light; different searchlights make us see "with different eyes." Searchlights are like "inventions" that may lead to "discoveries." Only research can tell us which searchlights reveal real facts.

Obviously, those new facts already existed before our searchlights brought them to light, but we cannot say much about what is still in "darkness." Yet, reality is beyond our control, for it is the touchstone of what we claim to know. That's why reality can never be fully captured by our knowledge, since it moves ahead of us like our horizon. All reality is knowable by the human mind, but not all of reality is actually known.[6] The result of this rather technical discussion is that reality has different aspects and appearances to show, which can be equally real, valid, and objective. Think of walking around a statue; what we see in the back is different from the front, not because we *wish* the back to be different but because the back *is* actually different from the front. In a similar way, there are many perspectives and outlooks on the world surrounding us, making for different points of view, different conceptual frameworks, different aspects of reality, different facts—all of which can be equally "real," "factual," "objective," and "valid" (albeit not equally "tangible"). But each one offers only a one-sided interpretation of reality.

Let's apply this concept of reality to the issue of science and religion. Physics, for example, discloses only one of the many aspects of this world, its physical aspect, providing physical answers to physical questions phrased in terms of physical *causes* and effects. Physics may be everywhere, but it's surely not all there is. Biology offers another perspective, providing biological answers to biological questions in terms of physical *causes* and biological *functions*. However, those who search only for causes or functions can never discern God. So, then, does God not exist? Of course he does; but we cannot see God when we come in from the wrong angle. Thank God there are more angles!

---

6. *CCC*, nos. 2467, 2500.

Since religion is about the origin and destination, the meaning and purpose of this world, religion sees the world from a religious perspective by discerning a heaven behind this earth—God's hand at work, so to speak. Religion brings us a miraculous, marvelous, wonderful world. After all, this is our Father's world—and therefore, a purpose-driven world. And yet it remains the very same world that we live in—no matter whether we look at it from a religious or a scientific viewpoint.

This is not to deny that God can only be seen and experienced by those in search of—and with an eye for—grounds, purpose, and meaning. Even though these are beyond the scope of scientific goals, they are no less "real," " factual,"" objective," or " or valid."There are many more perspectives than what science tries to cover with its barometers, thermometers, and spectrometers. We shouldn't close our eyes to what science has left untouched. We may reject what lies beyond science's horizon, but we can't actually reject or deny it, though we may try. That would be like denying or rejecting everything that could not be tested with a thermometer. Stephen Jay Gould put it this way: "Science can work only with naturalistic explanations; it can neither affirm nor deny other types of actors (like God) in other spheres (the moral realm, for example)."[7] The German physicist Robert Pohl (the inventor of the solid-state amplifier) would conclude his classroom demonstrations by saying, "And that gives us all the more cause for wonder." Science always leaves open the grand question: "why is there something like this rather than nothing?" Shrugging our shoulders in disregard doesn't make that question vanish. After science has explained and predicted all it can, we might think there is nothing more to wonder about, yet some residue is always left behind—the ground of all that exists.

What, then, is the *ground* of all that exists? It is like the framework around a spider's web; without the framework, the web could not exist. Likewise, God as the ground of our being is the framework supporting the web of our lives. God is the One who supplies the framework in which "we live and move and have our being" according to Saint Paul (Acts 17:28). Without God, we wouldn't exist—just as fish wouldn't exist without water. However, God cannot be detected with scientific eyes. Because God is the framework that supports all there is, he cannot be found *in* science. But he

---

7. Stephen Jay Gould, "Impeaching a Self-Appointed Judge," *Scientific American*, 267 (July 1992): 118–21.

can certainly be found *behind* and *beyond* and *beneath* science—in the vacuum or residue science has left behind. We are grounded in him—otherwise we would perish. As Dietrich Bonhoeffer wrote in a letter from his Nazi prison: "God wants us to realize his presence, not in unsolved problems, but in those that are solved [in science]."[8]

When discussing the question "where do we come from?" we found that evolution tells us the story from a physical, material perspective by dissecting it into small pieces. Creation instead tells us the *meta*physical story of how everything ultimately depends on God and on the cosmic order he created. Whereas evolution tells us that everything comes from something else, creation tells us that everything would be a no-thing if it didn't come from God. An evolutionary world depends on God as much as would a static world. Evolution follows the laws as laid out in creation, but creation is the origin and destination of evolution.

Some people think that evolution has taken the splendor out of creation. They often feel robbed when science tries to explain creation in terms of evolution. Indeed, science does reduce things by explaining them in terms of some kind of cause. For instance, it reduces the rainbow to the refraction of light. But this reduction to causes doesn't mean that scientists don't feel wonder when contemplating the natural world. There is immense beauty and splendor in the laws that govern our world and in the design our Creator has placed upon the universe. Just look at the beauty of what the laws of evolution have produced: a bewildering diversity of organisms living together in a rich variety of well-balanced ecosystems. It is my own experience—and I hope it's yours too—that, from this confrontation between science and religion, between evolution and creation, God has come out, if possible, more exalted than ever—more glorious, more all-pervading, more creative, more purified, more divine, more loving. It is "as though God were waiting behind every door opened by science."[9] I still find it startling that, when Job asks God for some much needed explanations, God is only willing to talk about what he created—such things as the Pleiades and the wild horses (cf. Job 38).

Whereas worldviews suffer from megalomania by attempting to explain everything under the sun from a one-sided, all-inclusive, and

---

8. May 29, 1944.

9. *Address to the Pontifical Academy of Sciences,* November 22, 1951.

monopolistic perspective, our real world is a multisided entity, stretching far beyond our own narrow-mindedness and finite scope. Hence our world, and anything in it, can be looked at from many perspectives—that is, with different eyes. The physical eye sees colors in nature (otherwise one is color-blind); the moral eye perceives values in this world (otherwise one is value-blind); the religious eye discerns God's presence in this world (otherwise one is spiritually blind). Does only the physical eye discern reality? I would rather claim that all these "eyes" discern reality, but each one sees a different aspect of it.

To illustrate this, consider a simple example—our eyelid movements. We can explain eyelid movements from several angles, each one leading to its own kind of explanation, each one detecting another aspect of eyelid movements, but all equally "real." Those movements can be explained as a cascade of physical causes, but also as a functional reflex (blinking), or as an expression of emotions, or as a result of an intentional action (winking), or as a manifestation of moral responsibility, even as an expression of religious prayer and awe. What entitles us to deny the reality of any of these explanations?

Or consider the following scenario: An epidemic has broken out in a harbor city, and we want to ask how this could happen. Maybe a scientist, probably a microbiologist, discovered that the epidemic was caused by a *microbe*. A second scientist, most likely an entomologist, could find that a microbe-carrying *flea* caused the epidemic. A third one, a zoologist, learned that *rats* have escaped from a ship that brought the microbe-carrying flea into the port. Do these different explanations compete with each other? No, they just perform different explanatory jobs. Each one offers a different part of the total answer, seen from a different perspective. But the common thread in all these answers is that they deal with physical *causes*, making each of them a scientific explanation.

But not all questions are in search of material *causes*. Imagine that a police investigator discovers that the epidemic was planned by terrorists who deliberately brought a ship (carrying the rats, fleas, and microbes) into the harbor. Would this challenge the previous answers? Of course not. The police officer had another type of question in mind. He or she was not searching for physical or material *causes*, but for human *intentions*, which are as real as physical causes can be. This makes for an answer phrased in terms of *reasons*. Denying the reality of this approach could cause our society great trouble. And then there are *religious* answers—not phrased in terms of causes or intentions, but of grounds, purposes, and destinations. Some preacher in this harbor town might see this event as part of a much larger picture—a cosmic warfare, that is, raging within each of us to tempt our free will to make the wrong choice between good and bad, between God and Satan. It's God's aim for each one of us to attain heaven after death, whereas Satan's aim is to ensure that as many people as possible miss that eternal goal. It is the religious eye that sees all of history, including this terrorist event taking place in a simple harbor town, as a cosmic and constant war between God and Satan, waged daily everywhere—24/7. It explains how such people can follow "orders" stemming from sources far beyond their own. Only religious people see this dimension in history that historians usually miss.

My point is that all the previous explanations, though diverse, do not compete with nor contradict one another, but offer different explanations from various perspectives. So they can all be equally true at the same time. Scientists tend to think that *their* explanation is *the* explanation, but instead I defend a *pluralism* of explanations against the false claim that there is only one true cause and one correct explanation for whatever happens on earth. The religious answer of the preacher does not deny or contradict the other answers, but it puts the physical *causes* advanced by scientists as well as the human *intentions* suggested by police investigators in a different perspective—that is, in a perspective of divine *purposes* and *grounds*. Religion always thinks in terms of a much wider, transcending framework, in an attempt to discern "God's hand" or "God's plan of salvation" in human history and our lives. If everyone would see the image of God in everyone else, the world would be very different.

In talking about perspectives, I would like to introduce a pyramid as a visual representation of the many layers or levels reality seems to contain. The term "level" is an alternative way of talking about perspectives, but it may clarify some consequences. If I say, "I wanted to go, but my legs didn't let me," I am actually jumping between two levels—the level of intentions ("I myself") and the level of causes ("my leg problems"). Sometimes that's legitimate, as in this case, but often it is not: To say, "I didn't do this, but my glands made me do it" is only an excuse for dodging my moral responsibilities (unless I could prove that this excuse was also caused by my glands . . . ). Something similar happens when advocates of eugenics declare that genetic diversity among humans (at the level of causes) entitles us to also treat those humans differently in a moral sense (at the level of values), or when evolutionists claim that we cannot come from God (at the level of grounds) because we came here through evolution (at the level of causes). In either case, these people are not only jumping levels, but also confusing levels—which is logically unsound and totally unreasonable.

This pyramid may also help us to better assess the world around us. For example, what was the "driving force" behind Hitler's gas chambers? The cyanide-based insecticide *Zyklon B* did the killing—at the level of causes, that is. But wasn't there much more to it? Strong emotions of anger and hate, plus feelings of superiority, were all operating, but at another level. Further, these emotions were propelled and reinforced by elements on yet another level: reasons and intentions coming from a racist worldview. Is that the end of the story? No. There was also Hitler's immorality, his lack of sound moral values. Where did his immorality come from? I am not talking about genes and upbringing! The fuel behind all his convictions was some satanic force battling against God's creation—which is the role of Satan, the father of all lies, hiding behind the scene. So we have many factors occurring at many different levels—not all tangible, but all equally real.

The pyramid conveys another important message: science may seem to take our sense of reality down several notches, but don't let that fool you. Science operates at "lower" levels, but it has nothing to say about the "higher" levels beyond its reach, and it certainly cannot claim those levels don't exist. Each level in the pyramid adds a new dimension to the level below it, and consequently, none of these levels can be *reduced* to any of the lower levels. Moral values, for instance, cannot be reduced to mere rational intentions, emotional motives, vital functions, or natural causes (see 5.2).

It is also exactly because they are at different levels in this pyramid that evolution and creation cannot really bite each other. Religion tells us that God is the creator of the world (the Alpha and Omega), on one level, and science tells us how he does it, at another level. Since they operate at different levels, the question "*How* did life arise?" is very different from the question "*Why* did life arise?" Evolution answers the *how* question regarding creation, whereas creation answers the *why* question regarding evolution. So we shouldn't attempt to read the Book of Scripture as if it were the Book of Nature—that's jumping levels.

## 5.2 The Roots of Rationality and Morality

As mentioned above, evolution and creation cannot bite each other—but they cannot even exist without each other! It's clear that religion needs some kind of scientific knowledge about this world (no matter how basic), but more striking is that science in itself is also necessarily incomplete and thus couldn't exist without help from above. Let us look at this in more detail concerning two important issues.

Evolutionary theory is, by nature, a rational construct, but it cannot explain its own *rationality*. It is thanks to creation that human beings have been endowed with *rationality*. Without philosophy and religion, there would be no domain of reasons. To put it in a slogan: Without creation, there would be no rationality, and therefore no understanding. In other words, science without creation would be meaningless and baseless.

Evolutionary theory is, by nature, a nonmoral construct and thus cannot provide any *morality* on its own. It is due to creation that human beings have been endowed with *morality*. Without philosophy and religion, there would be no domain of values. To put it briefly: Without creation, there would be no morality, and therefore no responsibility. In other words, science without creation would be an aimless and worthless undertaking.

Let's start with rationality. Animals occupy a place *in* the world, but humans also take up a view *on* the world—which calls for rationality. Science, for example, is a highly *rational* enterprise of finding facts with the help of mental and rational concepts. Rationality is based on reasoning by means of mental concepts and on having reasons for what we think, including hypotheses and theories. Reasoning is pondering realities beyond that which we can experience through our senses. So it is thanks to rationality that we can understand and explain the world we live in, since it was created according to an intelligible plan accessible to the human intellect using the natural light of reason.

## *Rationality*

I mentioned earlier that in his autobiography, Charles Darwin worried about the reliability of his theory of natural selection. If it were true his very own theory came from a mind produced by natural selection alone, Darwin wondered whether "the mind of man [can] be trusted when it draws such grand conclusions."[10] Whereas Darwin concluded from this that we cannot trust anything we know about God, I would rather argue the opposite, that we cannot trust anything we know if there were no God. If one doesn't trust the existence of purpose in creation, one is logically prevented from having confidence in one's own purposeful activities—and reasoning is certainly one of them. How could rationality ever arise in a universe that lacks rationality? Would there be place for the human mind in a mindless universe? If there were no sense in this world, it makes no sense for Dobzhansky to say: "Nothing in biology makes sense except in the light of evolution."[11] So how do we get sense back into our universe? Where do we find reason for trusting our own reasoning? Let us see.

I think most of us would agree that rationality claims to be objective and strives for universal truths. However, such a position does not fare well with the evolutionists' claim that rationality itself is also the product of natural selection. Evolutionists want to make rationality a matter of mere biological functionality, and since rationality is considered functional, it would be favored by natural selection. As a consequence, our genes would only make us believe (yes, a shaky belief) that our rational capabilities have an objective foundation, but in fact they don't; their only foundation would lie in our genes. So we would end up with a collective illusion foisted on us by our genes. If this doctrine were true, rationality would be as fragile as the DNA material of which it is supposedly made.

Doesn't this sound like mental suicide? As we discovered earlier (4.1.2), we cannot have it both ways. If we accept the reliability of our biological knowledge, including evolution, we cannot conclude at the same time that all human knowledge is just a product of evolution. First we take

---

10. Charles Darwin, *The Autobiography of Charles Darwin* (Cambridge, U.K.: Icon Books, 2003), p. 149.

11. Theodosius Dobzhansky, "Biology, Molecular and Organismic," *American Zoologist*, vol. 4 (1964), 443–452.

rationality seriously, and then we break it down with rational means. If we use the saw of the evolutionary theory to cut off the branch of the human mind, we are in fact cutting off the branch we were sitting on. We lose any reason for reasoning. We have forgotten that science and its theory of natural selection in fact must *assume* rationality but cannot create it.

Modern society has been tyrannized by the despotism of *relativism*, which arrogantly asserts that we have been born blind and that truth is beyond our reach. Indeed, intolerance can take on many faces. Most people think *absolutism* is intolerant because it pretends to know "the" truth. Well, it doesn't possess the truth, but must listen obediently to the truth; truth has no other weapon than itself. Instead, one could easily make the case that *relativism* is actually the more intolerant, because it conceitedly rejects any claim of truth as unacceptable.

How, then, can rationality be founded? It's clear that rationality cannot be defended by using rational means, for that would amount to begging the question; rationality cannot possibly establish its own rationality. Nor can it be founded on science, for it actually enables science. Fortunately, because we do need some stronghold for rationality, divine help comes to our aid.

This divine help can come from philosophy (which can lead us to a Creator) or from religion (which can establish a faith-based relationship with this Creator). They both refer to the same Creator, but the God of religion is more articulated than the God of philosophy. It is only because of the philosophical and religious concept of creation that I can trust my mind and my reasoning. Without God, I would have no *reason* to trust my own reasoning. The ultimate source of intelligibility is a Creator God. It is he, and only he, who laid the foundation for rationality. Thanks to our Creator, we have a rational lawgiver who guarantees order, stability, and predictability, for it is the essence of rationality that there are truths built into us and into the world that reason apprehends (and revelation reinforces). It is only God who can provide his creatures with the power of reason. That is why Albert Einstein could ponder the thought of Kant, who said that "the eternal mystery of the world is its comprehensibility."[12] Indeed, it is an incomprehensible thing, a mystery, to the scientist, but not

---

12. Albert Einstein, "Physics and Reality" in *Out of My Later Years* (The Estate of Albert Einstein, 1956), 61.

so to the religious believer. Scientists just trust, perhaps willy-nilly, that nature is law-abiding and comprehensible in principle. On the contrary, the denial of God our Creator is an acid that eats away the foundation of rationality.

## Morality

Let us move on from rationality to morality. The ideology of evolutionism (with its slogan of "survival of the fittest") has painted a "scientific" picture of life's history as "red in tooth and claw." However, if evolutionism were a legitimate ideological enterprise, we would end up with a world without values, which would surely be a dangerous world. Indeed, many evolutionists have tried very hard to get rid of those nasty moral and ethical values. But to no avail.

Evolutionists think they can get rid of moral and ethical values by reducing moral *values* to biological *functions*. Take the example of incest. There is an almost universal human taboo on incest—phrased in a moral law that says "intercourse with close relatives is wrong and forbidden." Evolutionists, for their part, would point out that inbreeding between close relatives tends to bring out recessive lethal traits and other afflictions that lessen the offspring's reproductive capacity. Voilà, natural selection has been promoting a genetic basis for behavioral avoidance of intercourse with close relatives.

But is that really true? If we would accept that this moral value is rooted in our genes, we should ask ourselves why human beings would still need an articulated *moral* rule to reinforce what by nature they would not desire to do anyway. As it happens, far too many people are willing to break moral rules when they can get away with it. Just think of the responsibility that parents feel toward their underage children. Is this a natural, instinctive responsibility that was promoted by natural selection because it presumably improves the offspring's reproductive capacity? Apparently it's not, given that far too many parents try to ignore their so-called natural responsibility. In other words, we are dealing here with responsibility in a *moral* sense. Responsibility is not a genetic phenomenon, but a moral one. Or think of monogamy. If we were monogamous by nature (like some animal species, such as swans), we wouldn't need moral laws to protect family life. Yet, it remains a timeless temptation to make *moral* responsibility merely a matter of genetics and natural selection. But that's a dead end. Responsibility is a moral concept (that's why animals bear no responsibility for their actions). Though human beings evolved unequal (at the level of causes), we were *created* equal (at the level of grounds). That's why morality wants us to be treated equal as well (at the level of values).

Or think of this: "Hit and run" may be our animal nature, but morality has something to add to it: "Hit and *don't* run." We need moral values precisely because by nature we do *not* tend to act morally. If we were merely animals without morality, we wouldn't even be able to do anything awful out of meanness or cruelty, since these are *moral* notions. Instead, such actions would just be legitimized as part of our animal nature. If morality were reduced to following our natural instincts, we would be in real trouble. Morality, on the other hand, has an added dimension that goes far beyond our animal nature. Hence it shouldn't surprise us that morality cannot be established through science, because moral values are beyond its reach. So, if science cannot establish its own *rationality*, it certainly cannot provide any *morality* either, for morality is not a matter of causality, functionality, or emotionality.

So our conclusions about morality are similar to those regarding rationality. They both claim objectivity: As rationality makes for universal truths, morality makes for universal obligations and absolute values. Because of its absolute values, morality cannot be based on anything that is relative and nonmoral by nature; values are ends in themselves, so they can't be based on other ends, since that would undermine their absolute claims. Many have tried to do so, however. Utilitarianism considers something morally right depending on its effects—that is, if it leads to "the greater happiness of a greater number of people." And evolutionism, in turn, claims that morality is legitimized if it's the outcome of natural selection—which would make morality a matter of mere biological success, without any objective basis. If this were true, we wouldn't be morally obligated, but would only *feel* obligated; our genetic makeup would only have us *believe* that our moral obligations rest on an objective foundation—a collective illusion, so to speak, foisted on us by our genes. Again, such a foundation is as fragile as the DNA material it is said to be made of.

There is another way of getting to the same point. All attempts to reduce moral *pre*scriptions to natural *de*scriptions are doomed to fail because of what the British philosopher G. E. Moore termed the "naturalistic fallacy."[13] This fallacy consists in erroneously reducing a *moral* property (being good or right) to a *natural* property (being natural, functional, genetic, more evolved, best for the majority, or whatever). Therefore, it would be a fallacy to define moral notions in nonmoral terms. Scientific maps show us *how* to go to get somewhere, but they don't tell us *where* to go, not to mention where we *should* or should *not* go. The fact that something *is* this way doesn't mean that it *ought* to be this way. The fact that something is natural does not imply that it is also a moral value that ought to be enforced. The fact that other human beings are genetically different does not imply that we ought to *value* them differently. The fact that natural selection is "natural" doesn't entail that it also should be put into action as a moral duty (no matter what eugenics claims). Or reversed, if slavery, murder, prostitution, or what have you, helped us fit into our environment—in line with the dogma of evolutionism—there wouldn't be anything morally wrong with it.

In other words, there is no direct way from "is" to "ought," from non-moral notions to moral concepts, from natural facts to moral values, from the natural sciences to ethics, from description to prescription. Compared with facts, moral values have an added dimension and therefore must be derived from a different realm—from the kingdom of heaven—and, as a result, ought to be "done on earth as it is in heaven." Moral values are ends in themselves—not disposable means to other ends. They are God-given moral rules.

So we must conclude that morality can't be based on anything else. It's not rooted in our genes; it's not the product of natural selection; it's not the result of any legislation; it's not a scientific conclusion. It's not based on anything useful or beneficial such as "the greater happiness of a greater number of people." All of these substitutes are morally irrelevant, since morality includes a new dimension that only morality has access to. Morality is written in our hearts and minds, guiding us to make the right choices in life. Therefore it must be from "above."

So where do our moral values come from? Only from God! Thanks to God, we can trust our moral values and laws, our ethics, our morality. How could there be moral laws if there were no moral Lawgiver? He gave them to us when he planted the "tree of the knowledge of good and evil" in the

---

13. *Principia Ethica*, 1903.

garden (cf. Gen 2:9). Even the U.S. Declaration of Independence recognizes that our human rights are *God*-given rights—otherwise we wouldn't even have any: "We hold these truths to be self-evident, that all men are created equal, that they are endowed by their *Creator* with certain unalienable Rights, that among these are Life, Liberty, and the pursuit of Happiness" (emphasis added). They are divine birthrights. Without God, we would have no *right* to claim any rights. If rights really came from human beings, and not God, people could take them away anytime—and they certainly have tried many times.

In short, it is only through creation that morality becomes a domain of objectivity beyond our own limitations. Since morality has an extra dimension that science lacks, science can't possibly be the basis of morality. If science had the final say, natural selection would sift out the moral altruists so that only the morally ruthless would survive. Surely, morality needs a better foundation than this—and that's where creation comes in. Without morality, there would only be material consequences to our dealings, but no moral responsibility for our actions. In his book *The Brothers Karamazov*, Fyodor Dostoyevsky notes that without God, all things are permissible. Without the compass of morality, we would head down a dangerous blind alley. It would be a world without good and bad, right and wrong, good and evil. The French philosopher and atheist Jean Paul Sartre was right on one point: If atheism were true, there could be no absolute or objective standard of right and wrong, for there would be no eternal heaven that would make values objective and universal.[14]

Some people think that evil belongs to a superstitious world of black and white that we can leave behind. They think we don't *do* anything wrong, but things just *go* wrong (with our genes, hormones, or whatever). They consider evil to be some kind of disease located in a gene or temporal lobe. They even say that we can evade moral responsibility by blaming our glands or animal ancestry for the way we act. But morality is about choices we make based on moral values. As a consequence, evil is the outcome of a corrupted morality. If morality were reduced to following our "natural instincts," we would be in real trouble. Without morality, the genes from our animal ancestry would have full autonomy. Without morality, there

---

14. See John F. Haught, "A Strange Witness," review of *The Moral Landscape*, by Sam Harris, *America* (February 7, 2011).

wouldn't be anything like the unselfish behavior of *moral* altruism, but there would only be *socio*-altruism (helping oneself by helping those who return the help) and *bio*-altruism (helping to spread one's own genes by rearing the offspring of close relatives). At the very moment that we let self-interest become the driving force behind all our human actions, moral altruism is on its way out—and evil would take over, making evolutionism the ultimate winner after all!

In conclusion, rationality and morality have much in common:

❖ The rational and moral capabilities of human beings are unparalleled in the animate world; animals don't have rationality or morality. Dogs may appear caring and dedicated, but they don't feel any *moral* obligations. Chimps may look smart but they are not *rational* and they lack what we call common sense or sound judgment.

❖ From this it follows that rationality and morality didn't come down to us from our prehuman ancestors via our umbilical cords.

❖ Rationality and morality don't even seem to be the outcome of some evolutionary process, as they are not programmed in our genes. Had *rationality* been genetically programmed, we could skip many years of education and wouldn't need rules of logic, math, methodology, and language to help us think more rationally. And had *morality* been coded in our genes, we wouldn't need ethical rules for us to behave morally. The Ten Commandments may have been etched in stone, but certainly not in our genes.

❖ Rationality and morality are also alike in being objective and absolute, which entitles them to claim universal validity. They both defy relativism—whether intellectual or moral relativism. Had they been encoded in our genes, however, they would not have any objective, universal, and absolute validity; and as a consequence, we would never be able to distinguish truth from untruth, or right from wrong.

❖ You might think rationality and morality are something for *science* to explain, but the situation is actually reversed: *They* explain science. Philosophically as well as historically, it was on the basis of rationality and morality that science was able to emerge and prosper. These two concepts keep science alive and ethical. Science cannot control rationality and morality; instead, rationality and morality should steer science.

❖ We cannot even establish rationality by showing how *irrational* it would be to reject rationality, since that would presume some sense of rationality. Neither can we establish morality by pointing out how *immoral* it would be to reject morality, for that would already require a basic sense of morality.

❖ Rational rules as well as moral obligations are evident. It is plainly evident that there is order in this world and that like causes produce like effects—there is just no hard proof for it. It is equally evident that it is wrong to kill other human beings. So the question is where evidence comes from then.

❖ Rationality and morality are gifts of creation, not products of evolution; they come with our minds and souls that possess the rational power of our intellect and the moral power of our conscience—a pure gift from God, written in our hearts.[15] They are evident because they are God-given. Nothing else can explain why we are rational and moral beings. Without God, we have no *reason* to trust our reasoning, and we have no *right* to claim any rights. That's why atheism is an acid that eats away the foundation of all rationality and morality. When you take them away, we are only animals.

❖ So who decides then what is true and right? It's certainly not up to us to decide what is *true*; that decision depends on the *laws of nature* in the cosmic design. And it's definitely not up to us to decide what is *right*, for that depends on the *natural law* of the cosmic design. Decisions like these are beyond our control. All we have to do is obediently listen to what the cosmic design—God's design—tells us. But we shouldn't forget we also have been marred with rational fallibility and moral weakness due to original sin.

## Church teaching on rationality and morality

What we have discussed so far about rationality and morality is fully in line with Church teaching. Vatican II stressed the roles of both rationality and morality. As to man's *rationality*, it says "that by his intellect, he sur-

---

15. See *CCC*, nos. 362–368.

passes the material universe, for he shares in the light of the divine mind";[16] and regarding man's *morality*, it states that "in the depths of his conscience, man detects a law which he does not impose upon himself, but which holds him to obedience."[17] Without God—that is, without the origins and destinations of creation—there would be no understanding or rationality, and no responsibility or morality. We were designed to know the truth and choose the good. Yet, we all know from experience that there is something wrong with our grasp of rationality and morality. Sometimes, we just can't think clearly, but even if we do, we don't always follow through, and we fail to opt for what is *true*. Likewise, we can't always discern what is right, but even if we do, we don't actually do what we know is *right*. If we have been graced with rationality and morality, why do we fall into error and do what is not right?

The answer is off-limits for science and cannot be found in the Book of Nature. But the Book of Scripture has a clear answer for us. The Book of Genesis tells us that Adam and Eve decided, of their free will, to follow their own versions of rationality and morality, inspired by Satan. Instead of following the light of God, they let in satanic forces that blind us to what is true and right. Ever since, our rationality and morality have come under attack. Because of the Fall, we are permanently under the influence of good spirits and bad spirits. Don't take these as two eternal principles locked in permanent conflict (as held in the errors of Dualism and Manichaeism)[18]; Satan and other demons are fallen angels created good by God, but they chose sin.[19] We live under constant attention of both God and Satan—and Satan never sleeps. Strong *spiritual* forces are battling each other either to guide our *rationality* by illuminating the human mind, or to deceive our rationality by darkening the human mind. They're also out to either guide our *morality*, by encouraging the human will, or to deceive our morality, by crippling the human will. Whereas good spirits strengthen our *virtues* (such as temperance, faith, hope, love), bad spirits incite our *vices* (such as lust, doubt, despair, violence). The bad spirits want us to call "true" what's untrue, and "right" what's wrong. When calling certain people "misguided," that's exactly what we mean—they literally are mis-guided.

---

16. *Gaudium et Spes*, 15.
17. Ibid, 16.
18. See *CCC*, no. 285.
19. See *CCC*, no. 391.

As a result of the Fall, our sense of rationality and our sense of morality have been damaged. In their desire to rule their own lives, the first humans rejected being dependent on God and subject to God's laws of nature and morality. Since then, we are engaged in a constant battle between God and Satan. We need divine grace not only to accept what is true and right, but also to reject what is untrue and wrong. In creating us, God gave us the freedom even to reject the very Giver of that freedom. God respects our freedom so much that somehow he even needed Mary's fiat to have his Son be born as our Savior. Her yes counteracted Eve's no and allowed Mary to become the Mother of God. Indeed, because human beings have this decisive power to say yes or no to bad and good spirits, let's pray that we accept the true and right, but reject the untrue and wrong. Therefore, we must learn to discern which spirit is steering and driving us, so we may regain control over the rationality and morality that were originally bestowed on us.

Fortunately, we have a better purpose in life, a better destination! And moral laws and values are our compass; thank God we do have a moral code based on the natural law that was written in our hearts. However, it is because of the original sin that not everyone clearly perceives the natural law. That's the reason why, according to Saint Augustine, God "wrote on the tables of law what men did not read in their hearts."

In this context, I quote Blaise Pascal (1623–1662), a brilliant mind in science as well as an inspired man in religion (he was a Catholic philosopher who also invented mechanical calculators and was an authority in statistics and hydrodynamics; the physical unit of pressure—*Pa*—is named for him). Pascal once said, "It is dangerous to show man in how many respects he resembles the lower animals, without pointing out his grandeur. It is also dangerous to direct his attention to his grandeur, without keeping him aware of his degradation."[20] That's the timeless story of the glory and the scandal, and each day we have a choice to make between them. Thanks to our Creator, each one of us is not just an evolutionary nobody but rather a significant somebody. Although evolution didn't have humanity "in mind"—for it has no mind—our Creator did. Planet Earth may not be in the center of the astronomers' universe, but in God's eyes it certainly is. And humanity may not be in the center of the biologists'

---

20. Blaise Pascal, *Thoughts on Religion and Philosophy*, trans. Isaac Taylor (Edinburgh: Otto Schulze and Co., 1901), chap 1, VII.

attention, but it is unquestionably the apple of God's eye, the highlight of creation. All of this is so awesome that we cannot help asking God, "What are human beings that you are mindful of them?" (Heb 2:6).

## 5.3 The Elusiveness of the Human Mind and Soul

Science has been eager to answer the question "*When* and *where* did humanity arise?" But regardless of the outcome, the problem still remains: "*What* happened then and there? Science has no access to this matter; it cannot catch the "I" of the human mind and soul. Following Plato and Aristotle, many have debated the difference between soul (*psyche*) and mind (*nous*). I will stay away from that discussion and say only this: Mind and soul are both spiritual, even if you consider the mind to be the intellectual part of the soul; I would say the mind is the soul's eye, its light—or put differently, the mind is the power of the soul by which we know truth. However, when I use the word "mind" in this book, I am referring to all of them together: my self, my mind, my soul, my spiritual side. I will use "mind," actually, as a shortcut for "I."

This "I" is enigmatic. You may, for instance, think, "I cannot help what I do, as the activity of my brain cells is determined by physical and biological laws." However, it is your very "I" who is thinking this. Is such a thought also determined by those laws? Somehow, we are talking here at two very different levels. In my thoughts, I am always a step ahead of myself, or above myself—which has been called the "systematic elusiveness of 'I,'"[21] leaving science in the dust. So what is this systematic elusiveness of "I"?

### 1. The human mind can reflect on itself

When I ask, "Who am I?," I'm not trying to find out my own name, gender, or age. Instead, I am searching for something behind these personal details—something unique that belongs only to me. Yet, I cannot put my finger on what this "I" stands for. It is like my shadow—something I cannot grasp.

Here we come in touch with an astounding capability of the human mind—the capacity of reflecting upon itself. I may notice, for instance, that

---

21. For instance, by Gilbert Ryle, albeit in a derogatory sense, in his book *The Concept of Mind* (London, Hutchinson, 1949).

I am clumsy; I may even notice that I am laughing at myself for being clumsy; and then I may decide to tell others that I noticed how I was laughing at my own clumsiness. This is an iterative or recursive process of self-reflection, making "I" act like my own shadow. I can never get away from it in the same way that I can get away from someone else's shadow. When I reflect on myself, it's always "I" doing this. A missile cannot be its own target, and your index finger cannot point at itself. But I can think about myself, correct my own actions, comment on my own actions, and even revise the comments on my own actions. In short, I have this unique desire to learn about myself through self-reflection.

We have a fascinating situation here: I-as-a-subject (I-now) can reflect on I-as-an-object (I-past). As a subject, I may investigate I-as-an-object and then realize, for instance, that I-as-an-object made a mistake. In contrast, I-as-a-subject is never open to investigation because its future possibilities are beyond its current actualities—and, therefore, I-now is always a pace ahead of I-past. I can remember my past only because I-now is more than I-past. That's why I can never blame my glands or my animal ancestry for what I do wrong, because I-now is always a pace ahead of I-past (including my glands).

Whenever I reflect on myself as an object, there is "some I" doing all of this as a subject. When reflecting further on this very "I," there is another "I" who is looking over my shoulder—and this can go on into infinity. Each time that I-now as a subject tries to catch I-past as an object, I-now stays ahead of the game, because I-as-a-subject is a necessary condition for comprehending any objects whatsoever, including I-as-an-object. We only know and understand objects because we form ideas and concepts in our minds, based on what we perceive through our senses. Put differently, the mind is not an object like other objects in this world, but it is their very origin as knowable; without the mind, there wouldn't be any objects of knowledge comprehensible to us. The human mind/soul is an elusive entity in this universe; no wonder it's called immaterial and spiritual.

## 2. The human mind can transcend itself

When I say or think: "I am only human," I am not comparing myself with something "below" me (such as a cat, a dog, or an ape), but I am comparing myself with something—or rather Someone—"above" that transcends me. When I call myself "only human," I am actually comparing myself with Someone who does not have the limitations I experience. In some mysterious way, I am reaching into the realm of the Absolute, far beyond myself. In so doing, the finite catches a glimpse of the Infinite. Somehow, I share "in the light of the divine mind," in the words of Vatican II. However, the human mind needs to be properly fed, for an unfed mind devours itself.

Of course, I cannot transcend myself on my own, but because I myself am made in the image of God, I perceive more than myself whenever I perceive myself completely. In this process, I may become more like God. Apparently, *Homo sapiens* is also a *Homo religiosus*. The "I" detects a "Thou" whose name is "I AM." But don't confuse the humbleness of your "I" with the grandeur of your ego as promoted by humanism. "Ego" arrogantly dominates, whereas "I" humbly reflects and corrects. "Ego" has forgotten who "I" is. My brain may make me a genius, but my mind could turn me into a sage.

Indeed, the human mind has an amazing ability to reach beyond its own body, or even beyond the universe. It can only do so if the human mind is a replica of the Creator's Mind. Since we were created in his image and likeness, we are endowed with rationality and morality, which sets us apart from the rest of the world. Here we stumble upon another elusive part of the human mind and soul. No wonder evolutionists are out to destroy this human image, because it's a divine image, a reflection of God's image. Our very humanity is at stake here. No wonder science had to drop out of the race long ago, for even if science wants to study the human mind, it needs to start from the minds of those very scientists. So biology can never fully comprehend the human mind, because biology itself depends on the working of the human mind. Isn't that mind-boggling?

## 3. The human mind is personal

The mind is always the mind of some specific person; it can never be in two persons, no more than a piece of wood can be in two places at once. The world of the mind is a *private* world. Mental events happen in my private world that is exclusive to me; no one else has direct access to this world. Whereas the world of my *body* is public and accessible to others, the world of my *mind* is private (but remember, the human being is a union of body and soul). Through introspection and retrospection (which are basically the same: I-now reflecting on I-past), I have access to my own private world in a way no one else does. Even brain scans have no access to my private world. They can only pick up brain waves—never my thoughts, as those cannot show up on pictures and scans. The German philosopher Gottfried Leibniz suggested picturing the brain as so enlarged one could walk in it as in a mill. Inside, we would only observe movements of several parts, but never anything like a thought. Hence thoughts must be different from physical movements and parts.

Nevertheless, it remains a timeless temptation for scientists to reduce the mental to the neural—which amounts to the nothing-buttery claim of reducing *mental* states of the mind to mere *neural* states of the brain; put in the words of the DNA co-discoverer Francis Crick: "You're nothing but a pack of neurons."[22] However, the mind doesn't go away when we try to explain it away. Picture yourself watching through a mirror while a scientist is studying your opened skull for brain waves. The philosopher Ludwig Wittgenstein noted correctly that the scientist is observing just *one* thing, outer brain activities, but the brain's owner is actually observing *two* things—that is, the *outer* brain activities via the mirror as well as the *inner* thought processes no one else has access to. To make the connection between "inner" *mental* states and "outer" *neural* states, scientists must depend on information that only the brain's owner can provide. And if you argue that the same holds for pain, I would say that pain can be induced physically, whereas thoughts cannot.

## 4. The human mind and its thoughts

Now we can consider another element of the mind: our thoughts. If seeing and hearing are physical acts, why not thinking? Well, thoughts are always *about* something, some mental object—no matter whether this something is real or make-believe. We don't just think, we always think *something*. This is what sets thoughts apart from what is physically going on in the brain. That is why it's basically impossible to identify mental events with neural events.

Some have argued that the brain works in the same way as a computer, because both use a binary code based on one (1) and zero (0). Neurons

22. *The Astonishing Hypothesis* (New York: Charles Scribner's Sons, 1994), 3.

either do (1) or do not (0) fire an electric impulse—in the same way as transistors either do (1) or do not (0) conduct an electric current. So the assumption is that the brain thinks like a computer "thinks." However, this analogy doesn't hold. If it were true, mental thoughts would be just a stream of binary code. Our thoughts may have a material substrate that works like a binary code, but it would not really matter whether this material substrate works with impulses (like in the brain) or with currents (like in a computer), because this material is only the physical carrier, a vehicle that carries something else—in the way trains can transport people or goods. One and the same thought can be coded in Morse, Braille, hieroglyphics, impulses, or whatever code language; it doesn't matter, for these codes are just physical carriers or vehicles. So it seems to me that the carrier doesn't create thoughts but merely transports them. The thoughts somehow use the vehicle.

However, once we acknowledge that the same thought can be transported by different vehicles (such as pen strokes, sound waves, cogwheels, currents, impulses), we realize that a thought must be different from its carrier. If I break my radio, the news report may stop, but not because the news was created by the radio; it was only the carrier that broke down. So what sets the thought apart from its carrier? Thoughts are more than a binary code; they also have sense and meaning, and that's what the binary code carries. Thoughts are *about* something else, something mental that is something beyond themselves. A computer lacks this very about-ness. Anything that shows up on a computer monitor remains just an empty collection of ones and zeros until human interpretation gives sense and meaning to the code. Similarly, a picture may carry information; but the picture itself is just an image on a piece of paper that only makes sense when a human being interprets it. In the same way, books provide lots of information for bookworms, but to real worms they only have paper to offer. Even a bank note would just be a blank note, a worthless piece of paper, if humans didn't have a mental conception of money.

Although some people think that a man is just a machine, instead we end up with something like a "man using the machine," for without human input, machines are meaningless tools. Without a human *subject, objects of knowledge* don't have any meaning, don't make any sense, and don't even exist—for these objects are based on mental concepts in the human mind. Without a human mind as a subject, there wouldn't be any mental objects at all. (The objects themselves would exist in reality, but they wouldn't be known by a human mind.) Computers, radios, and other forms of communication don't have meaning or sense until a human subject uses them as carriers of information. What's more, without a human subject, a computer doesn't even have a binary code, just two different states (on/off) that a human subject *uses* as a binary code (true/false) in order to carry and convey information that makes sense to other human subjects.

No wonder computers only do what we, human beings with a mind, make them do, for we have proven to be champion machine builders. A computer may play chess better than any chess champion, but it plays the game for the same reason a calculator adds or a pump pumps—because it is a machine designed for that purpose, not because it wants to. A machine doesn't have an "I" behind it (other than the "I" of its maker). No matter what I think when I am thinking, it is always "I" who am thinking something. Somehow, we are back to that famous systematic elusiveness of "I" again.

## 5. *The human mind and self-expression*

Next, consider self-expression. The human mind has an astounding capacity of expressing itself in various forms of art—literature, paintings, music. These expressions date from earliest human history. Of all animals in prehistory, only humans left behind stones with inscriptions, as well as the astonishing art in prehistoric caves.

Understandably, evolutionists originally considered such paintings as later forgeries, because they could not accept such a high level of self-expression so early in human history. I would retort: Even a caveman can do it! Some of the first Cro-Magnon sites, over 30,000 years old, have even yielded evidence for music: multiholed bone flutes capable of producing a remarkable complexity of sound.

We also see evidence of elaborate burials. The great effort put into the artwork found in prehistoric graves suggests that decoration and art were an integral part of the lives and societies of the people who made them. Besides, burial of the dead with material goods indicates a belief in an afterlife, for the goods were considered useful to the deceased in their future lives. How far had these people come, given their animal ancestry! How different this is from female apes that keep carrying their dead newborn around for quite a while, without having any idea of what is going on, until they finally give up and drop the dead remains. In Guinea, West Africa, for instance, chimp mothers have been seen in nature carrying and grooming their offspring's lifeless bodies for up to sixty-eight days. By the time the corpses were finally abandoned, the bodies had mummified and smelled of decay. But evolutionists give this observation their own twist: These must be sixty-eight days of actually *mourning* the dead! All I can say in reply is that only human beings could come up with such an explanation. These were not days of mourning but of ignorance. And why then is there no burial and grave? As I said before, only the "finite" human mind is able to catch a glimpse of the Infinite.

Only humans are able to laugh and cry—which is another sign of self-expression. Crocodiles may shed tears while devouring their prey, but it's certainly not due to remorse. Why are tears of laughing and crying so unique to human beings? The answer is again that only humans have self-awareness and can therefore express themselves this way. If some say that we developed these human features only by mimicking others, then why don't our pets look and act like us?

## 6. The human mind and self-determination

Finally, another striking feature of the human mind is its capacity of self-determination. Unlike animals, human beings have a strong desire of becoming someone of their own making. True, animals may have drives, impulses, instincts, or motives, but these are different from intentions or reasons, and they are always directly or indirectly related to sex or food (that's why behavioral experiments with animals usually involve mediating behavior with food rewards). Humans, on the other hand, have many more kinds of goals in life. Not only do they live their lives based on role models, but they are also guided by reasons, plans, beliefs, hopes, and dreams; and these shape them the way they are going to be. This is quite different from the way animals act. In the course of its life, an animal doesn't change much, but just looks and acts older. Humans, on the other hand, may have gone through dramatic changes in outlook on life, attitude, career, wisdom, faith, and/or beliefs—and hopefully for the better.

What's more, human self-determination is controlled not only by rationality but also by morality. Not everything that's thinkable or possible or reasonable is also permissible. Animals, in contrast, don't have any ethical values, so they follow whatever pops up in their brains. The relationship between predator and prey, for instance, has nothing to do with morality; if predators had a conscience guided by morality, their lives would be very tough. Animals never do awful things out of meanness or cruelty, for the simple reason that they have no morality—and thus no cruelty or meanness—but humans definitely have the capacity of committing atrocities. On the other hand, if animals do seem to do awful things, it's only because we consider their actions awful according to *our* standards of morality.

This fact has serious consequences for our attitude toward animals. Animals are certainly God's creatures, too, but since they don't hold moral values, they have no duties and responsibilities, and consequently no rights either. If animals did have moral rights, their fellow animals would have the moral duty to respect those rights as well—but they don't. Dogs may act as if they are caring, but they just follow their instinct; instinct may look like a sense of duty, but don't confuse this with *moral* loyalty. Dogs happen to have this instinct, whereas cats lack such an instinct, because it's not in their genes.

Humans, on the other hand, do have moral values, and because they do, they have to treat God's other creatures humanely and responsibly—not because animals have rights, but because humans owe it to God and to themselves, being stewards of God's creation. If humans were mere animals, as evolutionists proclaim them to be, humans would not have any morality either—that means they wouldn't bear any duties, and therefore not have any rights. Humans have rights only because they are God-given, not manmade. Human rights are not something due to us, but they are purely and solely given by God (and that's why others should respect them). But don't forget that rights come with duties—duties to God, to other humans, and therefore also to animals.

Since human beings do have value-regulated minds that work with a conscience, we are responsible and can be held accountable for the persons we are or the persons we have become. The nagging of one's conscience won't go away if one ignores it long enough. The image of one's self is a reflection of Someone Else in Whose image and likeness we were created. As Saint Irenaeus said in the second century, "Man is rational and therefore like God, he is created with free will and is a master over his acts." Because animals lack any kind of self-determination, not to mention any kind of morality, they don't live under the influence of good spirits that strengthen *virtues* (such as faith and hope), or of bad spirits that incite *vices* (such as doubt and despair). Because animals don't live on faith and hope, they don't die from doubt and despair. Dogs may look depressed and reject food, but that's a biological response at the level of emotions. Suicide, on the other hand, occurs at the level of reasons and intentions, allowing one to choose death over life. Animals don't throw themselves under trains or off bridges.

Pope John Paul II once said that "the human soul, on which man's humanity definitively depends, cannot emerge from matter, since the soul is of a spiritual nature."[23] It is this spiritual nature that gives the mind self-determination, so we are no longer at the mercy of our genes—for ultimately, it's not anatomy or DNA but the spiritual mind that makes a being *human*. Our model is in heaven, not on earth.

## Conclusions about the human mind

So we are back to this "systematic elusiveness of 'I'" that appears to be so uniquely human. Even if we ever fully understand the human *brain*, we will never fully understand the human *mind*, for it requires a mind to understand the brain, and it requires a human subject, a soul, to study any objects. It requires a *subject* to make sense of pictures or words, so they become *objects* of knowledge based on mental concepts. Without "I" as a subject, those items are meaningless and don't make any sense. It is obvious now that the knowing subject must be more than the known object, just as the projector is more than the projected images and a copy machine is more than the copies it makes.

So we have come to an important conclusion: When trying to study human consciousness, scientists make the human mind an *object* of science, but at the same time, the human mind is also the *subject* of science—for without the human mind and its rationality there would be no science at all. One needs a mind before one can study the mind! Biology can never fully comprehend the human mind because biology itself depends on the working of the human mind. How could the brain ever study itself? That would be like the miracle of a projector that projects itself; a hand that

---

23. General audience, April 16, 1986.

draws a hand cannot produce the very hand that does the drawing. It always amazes me how evolutionists like to downgrade the human mind while touting their own minds. Besides, if thoughts were merely the product of bodily and other natural actions, all thoughts would be equivalent, and we would have no way of telling the true from the false, or knowledge from error. That takes us back to the question: Can science be trusted if it is done by a mind that science has found to be the result of natural selection? Again, the answer is no—unless we are ready to derive the rationality of human beings from a Higher Source. And that's where we surely need divine help.

We need divine help for another reason. Along with the grandeur of self another side always exists, namely, its degradation. Ever since the original sin, we feel the constant temptation of turning "I" into "Ego," of replacing self-awareness with self-centeredness, of confusing self-determination with self-sufficiency, of exchanging virtues for vices—in short, of refusing to be the image of God. Because of the Fall, the human mind is at all times susceptible to spirits that either grace us with virtues or lure us into vices. Therefore, I must learn to discern which spirit is steering and driving me, so I may regain control of the self God has given me. Otherwise I won't proclaim what is true and seek what is right, although my Creator has given me the *power* to apprehend what is true and to discern what is right.

## 5.4 God's Presence in His Creation

So far, this book has said a great deal about science and its workings. Science always searches for material factors—physical causes and biological functions. Consequently, it portrays the world as a universe of closed physical causality. The universe is a complete whole that cannot be causally defective. So we might wonder how God could ever work within the seemingly closed causality as assumed and described by science and evolutionary theory. This leaves a few important questions: How can we talk about a transcendent God working in our natural world? How can God still be involved with the process of evolution that science tries to decipher, without his becoming a part of it? The Bible keeps repeating that God does act in this world and continues to act in human history. Over the centuries, he spoke through the prophets; he worked miracles; he sent his own Son to become man; he raised Jesus from the dead. If God is so active in the supernatural order, producing effects that are publicly accessible, it is difficult to rule out his involvement in the natural process of evolution. Why should God be capable of creating the world from nothing (*ex nihilo*), and yet be incapable of acting within the world once he has brought it into being? But again, how can he act in his creation without becoming a causal, physical element of it? How can the *Primary* Cause act in our world without becoming a *secondary* cause?

To solve this seeming enigma, I start from an often overlooked statement by Saint Thomas Aquinas: "God is [related] to the universe as the soul [*anima*] is to the body."[24] Notice that Aquinas did not say, "God is the soul, and the universe is the body" (which would be pantheism). In his words, Aquinas used the analogy of a person—that is, the relationship between mind/soul and body—to portray the relationship between God and world (i.e., by way of analogy).

I won't go into the difficult discussion of whether the concepts "mind," "spirit," and "soul" are different and how they would differ. In this chapter, I will lump all three together under the term "mind," taken as a non-material, spiritual entity to be at least distinguished from the material entity of the human body.

So we need to tackle the problem of mind and body (or soul and body) first, before we can go into the relationship of God and world. Let us use our previous distinctions again. Science speaks of the body in terms of material causes and functions, whereas we refer to the mind as the intellectual part of the soul in terms of nonmaterial reasons (rationality) and moral values (morality). So we can rephrase our question: How can a nomaterial, spiritual mind or soul work in a material, physical body?

A person appears to us as a *unity* of mind and body. Why do we distinguish them then? Well, the human mind certainly does not belong to the category of all kinds of bodily functions. Thinking, for instance, is undoubtedly a mental activity, which is different from functions like eating and running. Bodily activities are undeniably related to each other by *physical* connections; a lot of running physically makes us hungry. Mental activities, on the other hand, are not physically but *mentally* related. Thinking of "two times three" doesn't physically cause the thought of "six"; if it did, we probably could have skipped many years of school. The previous section showed

---

24. *Lectura romana in primum Sententiarum Petri Lombardi* 2, 17, 1, 1.

us that books, radios, televisions, and computers do not produce thoughts, nor do brains, that all of these are merely carriers that transport thoughts. Thoughts somehow *use* such vehicles, and therefore must surpass and transcend them.

How are mental activities and bodily activities related to each other? Since the mind is not found on the physical, scientific map of the body, it may seem to be nowhere in the chain of bodily activities, yet it is the "soul" of it all and pervades the entire body. It is part of everything the body does without being a bodily part. At this point I can only say that the physical and the mental appear to us as two different aspects or two different levels of some underlying reality—but that doesn't really explain much.

Thus, the mystery remains. Obviously, body and mind don't have a mental relationship; on the other hand, it's not a physical relationship, either. Thoughts may make you cry, but certainly not in the physical way that an onion makes you cry; and crying may make you think, but there is certainly not a physical causation here. We should never degrade the mind's activity to a physical link in a network of physical causes between neurons, muscles, and so forth. If thoughts were really the product of bodily actions, all thoughts would be equivalent, and we would have no way of telling truth from falsehood, nor knowledge from error. Apparently, the mind is not one of the players on the neuronal scene, but instead it is the author as well as the producer *behind* this neuronal play.

Yet, the mind does interfere with physical causes, but it does so in a rather mysterious way. What the intention of winking adds to the act of blinking is definitely not of a physical nature. Nevertheless, the mental and physical aspects affect each other in a way similar to how mass and gravity affect each other. We just do not know the mechanism of their interaction. I am certainly not promoting a dualism of mind and body, for the human person is a composit unity of mind and body. [25] What I am trying to stress is that the "knowing subject" is "more" than any "known object." All knowledge of objects is based on a subject that apprehends those objects, but the subject itself can never be fully captured by making it an object. Therefore, I consider body and mind to be two aspects of the same human being; you can *tell* them apart, but you can't *set* them apart. Their interaction is part of the cosmic design of creation, but we do not

---

25. See *CCC*, nos. 362–368.

know how the brain mediates our understanding. But no matter what or how, humans definitely alter themselves and their surroundings through the decisions they make and the values they hold in their mysterious minds. Thoughts can and do move the world as we all know. But how can this possibly happen?

An example from sports may make this issue more tangible. When golfers or baseball players hit a ball, they apply the laws of physics—that is, they use a specific force at a certain angle with a specific impact, leading to a cascade of physical causes and effects. Yet, much more goes on in this process—these players have a specific intention in mind, which eludes and transcends the laws of science. Do they go *against* natural laws? Of course not, but they do go *beyond* those laws. People who can't look beyond those physical laws and causes completely miss out on what the game is all about. We can steer the laws of nature in a direction of our own choosing (that's what we do in technology, for instance).

Even when people have lost the use of their mental faculties through dementia, Alzheimer's disease, or some other cause, they haven't lost their mind or their soul. Instead, certain defects in the physical network of neurons, neurotransmitters, and so forth prevent the mind from working through bodily activities the way it used to, or usually does; it's like static in a news broadcast. The mind is prevented from functioning, almost as if it has been imprisoned. Therapy may often help such people stay in touch with their "self." Our earlier comparison with a radio is pertinent here. The radio doesn't produce news reports but just carries and broadcasts them. We shouldn't overlook what's behind the carrier.

In other words, my mind is the "soul" of everything I do; it is behind everything my body does. In that sense, we might say it is part of everything I do with my body, and yet it is not a physical part of my body. That's the enigma we have to live with for the rest of our lives, as we share in the light of the Divine Mind. As already mentioned, the human being is a union of body and soul, yet the way they interact is mysterious to us.

## *The relationship between God and creation*

Now we are better equipped to appreciate the more mysterious relationship between God and his creation. God is a transcendent Being, surpassing all creation—being the First Cause in Saint Thomas's terminology. God is the creator and preserver, the Alpha and Omega, our origin and destination. As we have seen, Saint Thomas used an analogy that throws light on this topic: God is related to the world as the human soul is to the body.[26] Elsewhere, Aquinas says that "the king is in the kingdom what the soul is in the body, and what God is in the world."[27] This analogy is only an aid to enhance our understanding of God, and therefore inadequate. But it helps us realize that human beings were created after his image and likeness, sharing in the light of his Divine Mind.

Perhaps Saint Thomas never developed this analogy much further because he feared the pantheistic dangers of making God the mind, and the universe his body. In pantheism, God would be absolutely and solely immanent in his creation, without remaining fully transcendent to it. Indeed, the use of analogies is always limited, and therefore a potential source of dangerous implications. One limitation of Thomas's analogy is that the mind does not create the body, whereas God is the Creator of heaven and earth. Another is that the body does not depend on the mind in the way the world depends on God. So we can't let the analogy mislead us. Nevertheless, its advantages seem to outweigh its disadvantages. So let's look at it more closely to better understand how God interacts with his creation.

The analogy suggests that God somehow works in the world as the mind and soul work in the body. God's intervention in nature and evolution is not a physical intervention in the way science understands it, but one similar to the way the mind interacts with the body—being part of everything without being a physical part of it. On the one hand, this analogy prevents us from thinking that God's activity is a physical, inner-worldly factor interfering in the physical process of evolution, as creationists and even ID theorists take it. On the other hand, God can still be involved with the process of evolution as science tries to decipher it—but without becoming a physical part of it. Just as architects are not part of their buildings, yet are part of every part of them (without keeping them in existence, though), so God is not a part of what he created, yet he is actively involved with each and every part of it. The analogy of the relationship between mind and body may help us see how God is the soul that pervades all of creation and thus is part of everything in

---

26. Ibid.
27. *De Regno*, 1, 12–4.

creation without becoming a physical part. The Primary Cause lets the secondary causes do their work, but the secondary causes can only do their work thanks to the Primary Cause.

That is why God can never appear from a quest for physical causes. It remains a permanent temptation, though, to consider God as some kind of physical, inner-worldly cause jumping in when and where (other) physical causes cannot (yet) do the job or seem to require adjustment—which would make him an inner-worldly actor on the cosmic stage. I think I have stressed enough that a controlling power outside the universe cannot show itself to us as one of the facts inside the universe. Nevertheless, we should maintain that God is the soul that pervades all of creation and is part of everything in creation—but obviously not in a subordinate, physical way. Neither should this be understood in a pantheistic way. God is not a causal agency—not even with a capital A—ruling the world like a musician plays the piano, because God is of an entirely different nature. God is not one of the players on the world scene, but he is the Author and Director of this cosmic play. God is not a physical element in human history, but he is its Framework—the Lord of history, keeping everything in the world (including its secondary causes) in concert.

Remember, religion tells us *that* God is the Creator of the world, and science tells us *how* he does it. Whereas the science of evolution only deals with physical causes, religion deals with the origins and destinations of creation. We could rephrase this as follows: religion deals with the purposes that God, our Maker, has in mind for us. He is the one who leads the way, for God is his name. When we focus only on the laws of science, we miss out on the beautiful play that is going on around us. Since God is the source and soul of everything, he is *part* of each and every cosmic event that's taking place, but without becoming a cosmic *part*. Creation is not a matter of physical causality, of launching a series of cosmic reactions at some remote point in time. Instead, God's creative activity in this world is a continuous process of being its ground and its soul, intimately involved with all that's going on. He is above as well as beneath the universe. He holds it in being by the creative act of his will.

So it shouldn't surprise us that God can be found in everything— according to the famous adage of Saint Ignatius of Loyola. God can be found in the birth of a child given to us, in the healing we received through medication, in the successes we could achieve in our lives, as well as in the paths of evolution. Everything is "for the greater glory of God," as Saint Ignatius said.[28] God works through all of these like our minds work in our bodies, in a way that necessarily eludes science—that is, mysteriously, yet powerfully.

So are all these achievements not our own doing? In a way, they certainly are, because things in this world do happen through natural processes based on laws of nature. In another sense, they are not, because all these achievements depend on God and are somehow channeled by God in a way analogous to the way the mind works in the body. Saint Ignatius said, "Work as if everything depends on you, and pray as if everything depends on God." That's why we should always keep praising and thanking God for our children, our health, our achievements, and our evolutionary roots. All of these may appear to be our own doing, but God is the one to make them really work. Just as we ourselves can use the laws of nature for our own intentions and reasons, God may very well work through natural causes and human intentions to achieve his divine purposes and plans for salvation. God does not go *against* his own laws, but he does go *beyond* the laws of nature by using them for purposes he has in mind for us. God can use anything for a better purpose, even when we manage to mess things up ourselves—and we do that constantly.

To quote Pope John Paul II again, "The evolution of living beings . . . presents an internal finality which arouses admiration. This finality . . . obliges one to suppose a Mind which is its Inventor, its Creator."[29] This "Mind" pervades all of creation—perpetually and continuously. A mindless universe would have no place for the human mind. If human beings, made after his image and likeness, can be scientists, engineers, artists, and architects, how much more so can God be all of these for his own creation—for let's not forget that our image is just that—an image, certainly not the original. Thanks to this image and likeness, the finite human mind is able to read tiny bits of the infinite Mind of its Maker through his creation. However, we should always recall what Saint Augustine tells us: "If you have understood, then what you have understood is not God."[30] God always surpasses our human knowledge and understanding of him. That's

---

28. *Ad maiorem Dei gloriam*, or AMDG.
29. General audience, July 10, 1985.
30. *Canticum Canticorum*, 2801.

why any analogy has its limitations: "Our human words always fall short of the mystery of God."[31]

## Our ultimate destination

So how should we understand the *destination* of creation? We can find the answer in the first creation account—humans were created "in his image" and likeness (Gen 1:27), that of their Maker. This statement also guides us to our ultimate end. We may be earthy, made from earth, but we are also heavenly, made in his image. God gave us roots as well as wings. But then something else has happened—namely, the Fall. After he gave the first humans rationality and morality, how disappointed God must have been when his "mirror images" didn't appreciate those gifts, didn't even accept them, but fell for his adversary. They wanted to be like God in the sense of next to God, but not under God; they wanted to be creators, not creatures, so they continued following the animal part of their nature, worshiped idols, and killed other humans. Obviously, rational and moral blindness had struck—original sin.

Fortunately, God constantly invites us to live out the true, original identity and dignity that have been ours ever since each one of us was created—in his image and likeness, God's look-alikes, so to speak. God keeps reminding us of all the potential he has given us, no matter how obscure it may seem, so each of us can ultimately become the person we are meant to be. In order to help us regain our original identity, God has become concrete and fully immanent in Jesus Christ, when he became flesh of our flesh, the new Adam, a servant, and yet our Savior. Jesus was God and Man in one person, so that God and Man might be happy together again. In the words of John Paul II, Jesus Christ is "the human face of God and the divine face of Man." God may not be a player on the world scene as you and I are, but he took on the main role in this global play—in Jesus Christ, our Savior, born of the Virgin Mary.

Ever since those crucial events took place in Palestine, we know that our true identity is no longer the old Adam, the Adam after the Fall, but the new Adam, the Adam after the incarnation. The old Adam is no longer the measure of all things, but the new Adam is. Immersed in the material

---

31. *CCC*, no. 42.

world, we often neglect our eternal destiny, and so we haven't lived up to God's expectations. Christianity sees history as a constant cosmic warfare between God, calling us to our destination, and Satan, pulling us away from that destination. No one can escape the constant attentions of both God and Satan. In this war, Christ is the leader of God's campaign, so we want to be on his side—for that is the only way God will be able to restore in us our original dignity. Christians read the past and the future in the light of this paradigm.

But, hopefully, we are on our way, until "Christ is all and in all" (Col 3:11). It is true, we did start our lives as the old Adam, but we are heading for the new Adam in Christ Jesus. On our journey, we need to be constantly remolded according to his image. So it is not man who is the measure of all things (as in humanism), but Christ; it's not the old man but the new Man. Put differently, human beings may look like has-been apes in terms of evolution, but they are also would-be angels in terms of religion. The Book of Nature may find our roots in the animal world, but the Book of Scripture declares us rooted in God as well, in his divine image, giving us divine dignity. No wonder the Letter to the Hebrews expresses utter amazement: "What are human beings that you are mindful of them" (2:6). But Psalm 8 gives us an answer, telling us about these human beings: "You have made them a little lower than God, and crowned them with glory and honor. You have given them dominion over the works of your hands" (Ps 8:5–6).

Only one question is more important than, "Where do we come from?" It is the question, "Where do we go to?" Knowing who I am and where I come from, I should be able to know where I am going. Through Jesus Christ, I have been given a new chance to become the person I am meant to be since the day of my conception. No wonder that, in Christianity, the only thing that ultimately counts is the salvation of each person. Whereas Satan tries to make as many people as possible miss that goal, God's plan is to get us there. Thanks to creation, we can see light at the end of the tunnel of evolution. We may not know what the future holds but we do know that God holds the future—for each one of us. Our model is in heaven, not on earth. Let's ask God then, in prayer, to start us in the right way, for we are hard to turn—very hard indeed.

The French philosopher and renowned atheist Jean-Paul Sartre (whom Fr. Bochenski, OP, once called "the most intelligent and astute atheist that history has ever witnessed"[32]) said something similar at the end of his life—something that must have been shocking to his own ears. Toward the end of his life, blind and in poor health but still in full possession of his mental faculties, this uncompromising atheist had a profound conversion. In the spring of 1980, he spent much time with an ex-Maoist, Benny Lévy (writing under the pseudonym Pierre Victor). The two had a dialogue in the leftist Paris weekly *Le Nouvel Observateur*. It is sufficient to quote a single sentence from what Sartre said during this dialogue: "I do not feel that I am the product of chance, a speck of dust in the universe, but some-one who was expected, prepared, prefigured. In short, a being that only a Creator could put here; and this idea of a creating hand refers to God."[33] Doesn't that sound like a profession of faith?

Throughout this book we have been asking, "Where do we come from?" We may be animals, having much in common with other animals, but we are also called to be more than animals. Just as other animals, so we too are born into the world, and yet there is more to it: we baptize our newborns, circumcise them perhaps, and celebrate their coming. Like other animals, we need to eat, but unlike animals, we say grace before meals, perhaps observe food laws, follow table manners, fast on certain days, share meals with friends, and even partake of the Eucharist. Like animals, we need material goods to live, yet we know there is more to life than that. We don't live on bread alone, so on Sundays we rest from our labor and worship God. Like animals, we die and return to dust, but we also surround our dead with rituals, bury them, keep pictures and other symbols of them, and pray for their souls. Like animals, we have to cope with *physical* forces—our genes, reflexes, instincts, drives, and whatever surrounds us—but we also have to deal with *spiritual* forces that try to either enlighten or deceive our rationality and morality. Just like other animals, we have a body with a brain, and yet we are also endowed with a mind that is an image of the Creator's Mind, giving us divine dignity. Our role model is in heaven, not on earth. It's not surprising that evolutionists have been trying so hard to destroy that human image—since it's made in God's image.

We don't have a very impressive pedigree; we trace our ancestors back to the dust of the earth and the animal world. Our belly buttons are a

---

32. Joseph Bochenski, *The Road to Understanding—More Than Dreamt of in Your Philosophy* (North Andover, MA: Genesis Publishing, 1996).

33. Jean-Paul Sartre quoted in the *National Review*, June 11, 1982.

lasting reminder of this fact. Yet we have another lifeline, reaching directly into heaven, because we have Adam and Eve in our family tree; and since they were created in God's image and likeness, so were we. We could also say that we came here *through* evolution, yet we came here *from* God—in the same way that our children come *through* us but not *from* us. We are earthy, made from earth, and yet we are heavenly, made in God's image. Evolution gave us roots, but creation gives us wings. We can spread our spiritual wings and fly, no matter how earthbound our feet seem to be. Our bodies may look apelike and will return to dust, but the Catholic faith promises us that our souls are angelic. We are born not to be part of the ending, but of the beginning. Better things lie ahead than any we may leave behind. Let's try then to live up to God's expectations.

Undoubtedly, the road from has-been apes to would-be angels does seem long and winding, but in Genesis 3:9 we hear the voice of an unrelenting God who keeps calling to us, "Where are you?" That Voice is our saving grace. God is the Alpha and the Omega; from him we come and to him we will return. That's why each one of us is, in Sartre's words, not "the product of chance, a speck of dust in the universe, but someone who was expected, prepared, prefigured." At last, Sartre, the blind old man, had been cured from his "mental myopia." I hope and pray that if it was needed, you have had a similar conversion as you made your way through this book. In Christianity, it is never too late for conversion. Sartre had finally seen a glimpse of the Light that Pope Benedict XVI has been speaking of so unrelentingly. May this Light be our light as well, so we can live our lives being drawn to his divine Light.

## DELVING DEEPER

### Untangling the Confusion About Values

Morality is peculiar. When we hear of a murder, our usual reaction is, "That's a crime; thou shall not kill." But imagine if this criminal asked us, "Why is it forbidden to kill someone; what is wrong with it?" We might not know what to say. That the act of killing is wrong is something we just consider to be evident. You might ask: How do you mean, evident? Indeed, once values come into the picture, we seem to be facing a real problem. Let's analyze the situation a bit further.

What does it mean for something to be called "good" or "wrong"? We can distinguish two very different contexts. Something can be good in relation to a given objective. Medical *rules*, for instance, are good for the purpose of medical care. I prefer to call them rules, norms, or standards rather than values; some call them *instrumental* values. Anyway, they are *relative* because they tell us what we need to do in order to attain something else. If anyone ever wonders why a certain act is good in this instrumental sense, we can explain it in terms of its objective: Does the act meet its objective? If it does, it's considered good.

In a moral context, however, "good" has a very different meaning. Whatever is called "good" tells us what we *ought* to do—no matter what, whether we like it or not, whether we feel it or not. In this case, we speak of real *values*. Values are *absolute*, because they tell us what we ought to do as human beings, irrespective of any other objective; hence they are often called *intrinsic* values. They make for universal, objective, binding prescriptions; they are ends in themselves—not means to other ends. Moreover, the end does not justify the means; means as well as ends must be moral.[34]

Moral values tell us which actions are right or wrong; they are properties of these actions. In calling certain actions good, we describe a moral property of that action, not just our feeling about it. But once we acknowledge this, we find ourselves dealing with three elements that need to be clearly distinguished:

❖ First, there is something that has a moral value (good or bad). The *act* of killing an innocent person would be such a thing.

❖ This act has a property that makes it right or wrong—that's when the *value* itself comes into the picture. Moral values and laws determine what is right or wrong.

❖ And then there are our personal feelings or discernments regarding values, which shape our evaluations. Here we are dealing with someone's personal *attitude* toward moral values, causing some to think morality can be determined by special interest groups or a majority vote.

---

34. See *CCC*, no. 1753.

The three elements we distinguished above should never be confused; the act is the vehicle of the value (having a value) and is very different from the value itself (being a value); and values, in turn, should be distinguished from human attitudes toward values (being valued).

These are clear distinctions. However, some people think that "having value" is the same as "being valued." In other words, they believe that in making evaluations, we create values according to these evaluations. So when evaluations change, the moral values and laws are said to change. Hence, evaluations—and thus values—would be utterly a matter of relativity, depending on the era, culture, and location of the person who makes the evaluations. In this view, values would be subject to change during the course of human history—determined by a majority vote, so to speak. Thus we end up with moral relativism—an absolute claim stating that there are no absolutes (except for this absolute claim itself, of course). Relativists reject any authority, but want to be the new authority. Utilitarianism, for instance, tells us that everything has to be weighed, because it is relative to something else; there wouldn't be any absolute values, for those could never be weighed. But how could "a great good" ever permit "minor evils," for how could good ever originate from evil? Even eugenics has been defended as being for "the greater good."

That's why moral absolutists emphasize that evaluations are merely a reflection of the way we discern moral values and react to them—in other words, evaluations of values should be distinguished from the values themselves. Absolutists warn us not to mistake our evaluations for values; whereas moral *evaluations* may be volatile and fluctuating, moral *values* and laws are eternal, objective, and absolute (like mathematical laws). According to the absolutists' view, we certainly can make moral mistakes, whereas moral relativists wouldn't acknowledge this.

I myself embrace the absolutists' view, which would entail that some among us are able to clearly discern certain values and evaluate them properly, whereas others are not. How do we justify those values? The only apt answer is, "They are just evident," or in religious terms "God-given," coming from the tree of good and bad, or in Catholic terms, "natural," rooted in nature as a natural law. Anyone who does not see their evidence is blind. Just as there are color-blind people, some people are value-blind.

Let me illustrate this point a little more. A few centuries ago, slavery was not evaluated as morally wrong, but nowadays it is by most people. Did our moral values change? No, they did not; but our evaluations certainly did. Only a few people in the past—Saint Anselm being one of the first—were able to discern the objective and universal value of personal freedom and human rights (versus slavery), whereas most of their contemporaries were blind to this value. Something similar holds for the value of monogamy; many people in the past were blind to this value (and some still are). As Jesus would say, "You have heard that it was said . . . But I say to you . . ."—meaning whether you see it or not, this is the way it is in this world.

Or take the following case: Nowadays, many people have become blind to the value that all human life, including unborn life, deserves protection. Only some see very clearly the absolute value of all human life, which makes abortion a morally wrong act. Does this mean their opponents are blinded and shrouded? People who have a clear discernment of the value of human life would say so. How often the people who had the clearest discernment of moral values were persecuted by the mass of blind people! Yet, humanity's progress often depended on these very people having a sharper and better discernment of moral values. Right now, we are very grateful for those antislavery activists of the past. Perhaps some day, most people will also be very grateful to the antiabortion activists. It's not the *values* that change in the course of human evolution but their *evaluations*— that is, our subjective attitudes toward these objective values. Objective values are not disposable.

Put differently, there is no room for pro-choice in morality (and even if there were, would it be the choice of the mother or of the unborn baby, I always wonder). Morality does not allow us to choose between pro-life and pro-abortion, or between pro-freedom and pro-slavery. Morality is not about the choices we have but about the choices that are *right*; it obliges us to go for pro-life and pro-freedom; otherwise we would make a moral mistake. Obviously, we are dealing here with objective, eternal, absolute values, no matter what our current, momentary moral evaluations may be like. As the Book of Deuteronomy puts it, "I have set before you life and death . . . . Choose life so that you and your descendants may live" (30:19).

## Morality Cannot Be Controlled by Biology

Some people insist that a moral value is nothing but a disguised biological phenomenon. Herbert Spencer championed this ideology when he equated "morally good" with what is "more evolved." Ever since, this idea has become a popular maneuver—adducing biological criteria to justify an ethical or moral judgment. What's "good" in a moral sense is said to be so because it is also "functional" in a biological sense.

However, there is a conceptual flaw. What is called "biological" or "functional" or "natural" does not have to be evaluated as "morally good" at the same time. There are no, or hardly any, societies where the *moral* order is a take-off from the *biological* "law of the jungle"—and even if there are, one may certainly wonder whether this substitution would be *morally* right (eugenics, for instance, would claim it is). Margaret Sanger, the founder of Planned Parenthood, made some scary statements on this issue: "The most merciful thing that a large family does to one of its infant members is to kill it."[35] Or: "More children from the fit, less from the unfit—that is the chief aim of birth control."[36] However, what is biologically "right" may very well be morally wrong. If some behavior is functional or natural, it does not follow from it that we have the moral duty to put it into operation. *Morality* is not a matter of *functionality*. Put differently, moral questions cannot be solved by giving biological answers, since those answers are based on morally irrelevant criteria. Science simply cannot provide or establish morality, since morality is beyond its reach and authority.

Consider the abortion debate. The value of human life has often been based on biological criteria, such as the extent of cerebral activity. The moral argument goes along these lines: The more cerebral activity there is, the more value a human life has, and, therefore, the more protection it deserves. However, the *biological* criteria adduced here are *morally* irrelevant. Besides, the right to life is a timeless *moral* right, whereas the right to vote, to drive cars, or to drink alcohol are all *legal* rights that only come into effect as we mature.

Abraham Lincoln used this distinction between moral and nonmoral when he asked people what made them think that enslaving others wasn't wrong. Is it because of their darker skin color? If so, he said, you might be next when someone with a lighter skin than you wants to enslave you. Is it because of a lower intelligence? If so, you might be next when

---

35. Margaret Sanger, *Women and the New Race* (New York: Brentano, 1920), 63.
36. *Birth Control Review*, May 1919, p. 12.

someone more intelligent than you wants to enslave you. . . . Lincoln's point is clear: All the answers you might come up with to defend your (seemingly moral) claim use morally irrelevant criteria. The same holds for the value of human life. This value cannot be based on or derived from *biological* standards, since these are by definition *morally* irrelevant. Moral values are ends in themselves—not disposable means to other ends. So in no way would "a great good" ever permit "minor" moral evils, for one can't do evil so that good may come. In morality, there's no "Thou shall not, *unless* . . ."

A morally acceptable alternative, on the other hand, would be a *moral* standard of old, saying that whatever is born of human beings is human life—irrespective of its extent of cerebral activity or the number of its "defects." This viewpoint would imply that all human life deserves protection—from womb to tomb, from orphanages to mental institutions, and at all stages of its development. Will there be any sanctuary left if even the womb of a pregnant mother is no longer a safe place?

We cannot and should not draw any imaginary line between prehuman, human, or post-human stages in life—a person is a person, no matter how small or stunted. This is the moral law that resounds through all of history (the so-called "natural law" in Catholic doctrine, which is not manmade but God-given Law). It has become even more explicit and refined in the Scriptures, and therefore has also been the age-old message of the Catholic Church: proclaiming the sanctity of all human life born from human parents. Psalm 139 so beautifully praises God for this: "You formed my inward parts; you knit me together in my mother's womb" (Ps 139:13). Obviously, we could say more, but that's beyond the scope of this book.

## When and Where Did Humanity Emerge?

If we do accept that the biological part of humanity was the outcome of an evolutionary process, that raises the famous—or should I say infamous—questions of "*Where* and *when?*": Where and when did the human mind—including its rationality and morality—surface? The first part, the *where* question, seems to be the easiest to answer. Based on skeletal finds, most paleontologists would point to Africa as our cradle. But when probing further, we get trapped into many difficult questions. Paleontological evidence is rather anecdotal and generally not very conclusive.

Fortunately, DNA research gives us better evidence, because it lets us trace through DNA what our (first human?) ancestors must have looked like. This is done by comparing the neutral DNA sections of two types of DNA: *mitochondrial* DNA (because it is passed unmixed from a mother to all her children, along the maternal line) and *Y-chromosomal* DNA (because it is passed unmixed from a father to all his sons, along the paternal line). All lineages are identified by one or more so-called DNA markers (rare mutations in noncoding DNA segments) that create a DNA signature or *haplotype* of their ancestry. These lineages are like ancestral clans and form *haplogroups* with some specific rare mutations, and then they split into subgroups that have some additional markers (or rare mutations). This kind of analysis allows us to construct a DNA family tree that has at its origin a mitochondrial Eve and a Y-chromosomal Adam representing our most recent common ancestors that have DNA markers like ours. Such a reconstruction tells us that these ancestors were living somewhere in Africa (which is consistent with paleontology). All other contemporaries of these protohumans failed to produce a direct unbroken male or female line to present-day human populations.

But we can't jump to the conclusion that we can finally locate in the Book of Nature the Adam and Eve from the Book of Scripture. The two genetic prototypes that science has come up with are merely two common ancestors who share the same rare DNA markers that we possess. But this doesn't mean they also represent the two individuals who launched the history of humanity and became part of *God's* history with humanity, once they were graced by God with rationality and morality. They are more prototypes than individuals. What the Book of Scripture tells us is always beyond the scope of the Book of Nature—but the two books can never be at odds.

Although this DNA approach confirms that humanity originated relatively recently in Africa, and not at several separate locations as some scientists had once claimed, it also has many limitations because it is based on several presuppositions (such as a certain, unchanging rate of mutation, or a lack of natural selection in neutral DNA sections). So we could give science some credit here, but always with due reservations.

The Church, for her part, has taken an unambiguous stand on this issue, stating that humanity started with *one* couple. Is this in conflict with science? Not really, for the simple reason that human beings become human only thanks to God, as he endows each one of them with an immaterial human soul that comes with rationality and morality. And this immaterial human soul is definitely beyond the reach of science and paleontology. I don't inherit my soul from my parents, and my soul certainly doesn't come with their DNA, nor did it come through the umbilical cord. So where do I come from then? The simple answer is as follows: My DNA comes from my ancestors, but my soul comes from God. The Book of Nature may be about our biological roots, but the Book of Scripture deals with our spiritual roots.

The second question, *when* all of this happened, is also controversial. Science only has access to the material substrate underlying the immaterial human mind. Since science can only go by physical appearances, scientists usually take the following four criteria into consideration:

1. Being a two-footer (biped) seems to be a big advantage for other human features—the main advantage being that the neck muscles put less restraint on the expansion of the brain. *Homo erectus* literally means "biped man," but does this designation make him/her a human being? Most scientists think that being a biped in itself is not enough to qualify, but this decision is rather arbitrary, and certainly not scientific.

2. Having a relatively large brain capacity seems to be necessary for most activities of the human mind. *Homo sapiens* is indeed the "rational man" who clearly has a relatively large brain compared to other mammals. Brain capacity has often been used as an important indicator for being human, but we have no idea where to draw the line. Besides, brain mass or quantity is not directly correlated to brain quality, let alone mental activities. And unlike the human brain, the human mind is a very peculiar entity, as we have seen.

3. The jaw of the skull needs to be proportionally small to allow smaller jaw muscles that free the brain to expand. In general, we do see a tendency for the brain part to increase while the jaw part decreases. But we do not know which development is the cause and which the effect, not to mention how else they may be caused, related, correlated, or connected.

4. The ability to make tools seems to be an essential characteristic of human beings. First, tool-making requires an opposable thumb,

which is a signature feature of most primates and was probably developed as an adaptation to arboreal life. Although many animals show (direct) tool use, only humans show *indirect* tool use (as in making a chopping stone to help shape a flint). Animals may be capable of using tools, but designing tools seems to come with a more complex (and perhaps larger) brain structure. *Homo habilis* is literally the "handy man," but should we consider him/her a human being? Who decides? Perhaps toolmaking is just a consequence of becoming an "intelligent designer."

Does all this make it easier for us to locate the transition point between prehuman and human beings in evolution? It might help, but it does not really aid us in assigning the proper status to specific paleontological finds. Notice how the aforementioned names of species all differ, suggesting they are separated by reproductive isolation—but we have no way of knowing that. Apparently, a lot of guesswork is going on, sometimes based on almost anecdotal evidence of a single fossil find, so we shouldn't place too much confidence in what scientists say. Even the DNA approach mentioned above has many limitations. In order for us to determine a time frame, we assume that DNA mutations in these noncoding DNA regions occur at a fixed rate (but do they?); that rates don't vary between markers (but they do); that mutations don't get repaired (but they may); and that they are not subject to natural selection (despite contrary evidence that mitochondrial DNA doesn't evolve neutrally, showing a lower diversity in colder climates, for instance). Consequently, estimates as to when these lineages appeared have varied from 30,000 to 400,000 years ago—which is quite a range.

My conclusion is that scientific answers to the *when* question are as uncertain as those to the *where* question. Besides, looking at skulls or DNA gives us no clue as to *when* and *where* our ancestors became endowed with rationality and morality as a gift from God. Pope John Paul II put it pithily, "it is possible that the human body . . . could have been gradually prepared in the forms of antecedent living beings. However, the human soul, on which man's humanity definitively depends, cannot emerge from matter, since the soul is of a spiritual nature."[37] That's the point where religion needs to complement science, because the human soul and mind—which form the core of humanity—are beyond the reach of anatomy and DNA.

---

37. General audience, April 16, 1986.

# Suggestions for Further Reading

Ayala, Francisco J. *Darwin's Gift to Science and Religion*. Washington, DC: Joseph Henry Press, 2007.

———, *Darwin and Intelligent Design*. Minneapolis: Fortress Press, 2006.

Barbour, Ian G. *Religion and Science: Historical and Contemporary Issues*. San Francisco: HarperCollins, 1997.

Barr, Stephen M. *Modern Physics and Ancient Faith*. South Bend, IN: University of Notre Dame Press, 2006.

Bochenski Joseph M., OP. *The Road to Understanding—More Than Dreamt of in Your Philosophy*. North Andover, MA: Genesis Publishing Company, 1996.

Collins, Francis S. *The Language of God*. New York: Free Press, 2006.

Dulles, Avery Cardinal, SJ. "God and Evolution." *First Things*, October, 2007.

Feser, Edward. *Aquinas: A Beginner's Guide*. Oxford: Oneworld Publications, 2009.

Gould, Stephen Jay. *Rocks of Ages: Science and Religion in the Fullness of Life*. New York: Ballantine Books, 1999.

Hahn, Scott. *The Lamb's Supper: The Mass as Heaven on Earth*. New York: Doubleday, 1999.

Hannam, James. *God's Philosophers: How the Medieval World Laid the Foundations of Modern Science*. London: Icon Books, 2009.

Jaki, Stanley L., OSB. *The Savior of Science*. Grand Rapids, MI: Eerdmans, 2000.

John Paul II. *Fides et Ratio: On the Relationship of Faith and Reason*. Boston, MA: Pauline Books and Media, 1998.

Kass, Leon R. *Toward a More Natural Science*. New York: Simon and Schuster, 1985.

Kitcher, Philip. *Abusing Science: The Case Against Creationism.* Cambridge, MA: MIT Press, 1982

Kreeft, Peter, and Ronald Tacelli, SJ. *Handbook of Catholic Apologetics: Reasoned Answers to Questions of Faith.* San Francisco: Ignatius Press, 2009.

Lonergan, Bernard., SJ. *Insight, a Study of Human Understanding.* London: Darton, Longman, and Todd, 1983.

Lewis, C. S. *Mere Christianity.* New York: Harper Collins, 2001.

Miller, Kenneth R. *Finding Darwin's God: A Scientist's Search for Common Ground Between God and Evolution.* New York: Harper Collins, 1999.

Miller, Kenneth R. *Only a Theory: Evolution and the Battle for America's Soul.* New York: Viking Penguin, 2008.

Polkinghorne, John. *Science and Theology: An Introduction.* Minneapolis: Fortress Press, 1998.

Ratzinger, Joseph Cardinal, *"In the Beginning . . . ."* Translated by Boniface Ramsey. Grand Rapids, MI: Eerdmans, 1995.

Schönborn, Christoph Cardinal. "The Designs of Science." *First Things,* January 2006.

————, *Creation and Evolution: A Conference with Pope Benedict XVI in Castel Gandolfo.* San Francisco: Ignatius Press, 2008.

# Index

# BOOKS & MEDIA

The Daughters of St. Paul operate book and media centers at the following address-es. Visit, call, or write the one nearest you today, or find us on the World Wide Web, www.pauline.org.

**CALIFORNIA**

| | |
|---|---|
| 3908 Sepulveda Blvd, Culver City, CA 90230 | 310-397-8676 |
| 935 Brewster Avenue, Redwood City, CA 94063 | 650-369-4230 |
| 5945 Balboa Avenue, San Diego, CA 92111 | 858-565-9181 |

**FLORIDA**

| | |
|---|---|
| 145 S.W. 107th Avenue, Miami, FL 33174 | 305-559-6715 |

**HAWAII**

| | |
|---|---|
| 1143 Bishop Street, Honolulu, HI 96813 | 808-521-2731 |
| Neighbor Islands call: | 866-521-2731 |

**ILLINOIS**

| | |
|---|---|
| 172 North Michigan Avenue, Chicago, IL 60601 | 312-346-4228 |

**LOUISIANA**

| | |
|---|---|
| 4403 Veterans Memorial Blvd, Metairie, LA 70006 | 504-887-7631 |

**MASSACHUSETTS**

| | |
|---|---|
| 885 Providence Hwy, Dedham, MA 02026 | 781-326-5385 |

**MISSOURI**

| | |
|---|---|
| 9804 Watson Road, St. Louis, MO 63126 | 314-965-3512 |

**NEW YORK**

| | |
|---|---|
| 64 W. 38th Street, New York, NY 10018 | 212-754-1110 |

**PENNSYLVANIA**

| | |
|---|---|
| Philadelphia: Relocating | 215-676-9494 |

**SOUTH CAROLINA**

| | |
|---|---|
| 243 King Street, Charleston, SC 29401 | 843-577-0175 |

**VIRGINIA**

| | |
|---|---|
| 1025 King Street, Alexandria, VA 22314 | 703-549-3806 |

**CANADA**

| | |
|---|---|
| 3022 Dufferin Street, Toronto, ON M6B 3T5 | 416-781-9131 |

¡También somos su fuente para libros,
videos y música en español!